THE ORIGIN OF DREAMS

THE ORIGIN OF DREAMS

Joseph Griffin

The Origin of Dreams
© Joseph Griffin 1997

The Therapist Ltd.
Chalvington, Hailsham, East Sussex BN27 3TD, United Kingdom

Cover painting by James Marsh.

Printed in Great Britain by Cromwell Press, Trowbridge, Wiltshire.

ISBN 1 899398 30 9

Dedication

To my wife, Liz, without whose support this book would not have been possible.

To my daughters, Mona-May and Liley Beth, who have shown me that some dreams come true.

To my good friend, Ivan Tyrrell, the editor of this book, whose lightness of touch and felicity of expression brought increased clarity to almost every page.

CONTENTS

Here we are, all of us: in a dream-caravan.
    A caravan, but a dream – a dream, but a caravan.
And we know which are the dreams.
    Therein lies the hope.

*Bahaudin**

* From *Caravan of Dreams* by Idries Shah

Chapter 1

THE ORIGIN OF DREAMS

An evolutionary puzzle

"Dreaming must be seen as something more than anomalous perceiving. It is a human conceptual achievement of the first magnitude and one of the core problems of cognitive psychology. Dreaming needs once again, as it was by Freud, to be recognised as a problem so central to the study of the mind that its resolution can help to reveal the fundamental structures of human thought."

Dr David Foulkes (Pioneer in Scientific Dream Research)

IN RECENT YEARS the recognition that a comprehensive understanding of human nature requires a holistic approach – a recognition of the interdependence of the biological and the psychological – has developed rapidly. It is commonly referred to as the 'mind-body' approach and has produced enormous advances in our understanding of the brain, behaviour, immunity and disease in the last ten years – as most elegantly expressed in *The Sickening Mind* by Paul Martin (1997). In *The Origin of Dreams*, you will discover how our understanding of human dreaming is also advanced by such an integrated approach.

Traditionally, theories that seek to explain why we dream tended to divide into two broad categories of explanation – psychological and biological.

Psychological theories are usually of a psychodynamic type, such as Jung's and Freud's, or of an information processing type, such as Calvin Hall's cognitive theory or Evans' computer theory. Psychological theories held sway in the first half of the century until, in 1953, Aserinsky & Kleitman discovered the special state of physiological arousal known as 'rapid eye movement', or 'REM' sleep, which appears to have a close relationship with dreaming. This gave a great boost to the biological approach to understanding the function of dreaming. Biological theories stimulated by this finding range from the Crick and Mitchison (1983) 'elimination of parasitic connections in the neural net hypothesis' (dream to forget theory) to the 'activation-synthesis' hypothesis of Hobson and McCarley (1977). All the main biological and psychological theories are reviewed in the following pages – the psychological theories in chapter 2 and the biological theories in chapter 3.

The need to integrate the biological and psychological approaches to account for the full complexity of human dreaming was apparent to Hudson (1985) when he wrote: "This evolutionary puzzle (dreaming and REM sleep) and the question of the brain's operating principles are tied together, as Crick and Mitchison correctly assume. What they do not entertain is the possibility of an altogether more sweeping synthesis and at the same time more rigorous explanation, in which these biological considerations are gathered together with another more strictly psychological one: the question of the formal properties implicit in the meaning of dreams themselves. In such a synthesis 'bottom up' and 'top down' theorising about the sleeping brain and its products would knit together, and the conceptual gap within psychology between mechanistic and interpretative modes of explanation would close... Such a synthesis is as exciting a prospect as any psychology now offers, and eminently achievable – although at present it hovers in mid-distance, still out of reach."

The biological research reviewed in chapter 2 clearly shows that there is a close relationship between dreams and REM sleep. Dreaming occurs primarily during REM sleep. The REM state occupies the greater proportion of sleep time in the foetus during the last trimester (eighty per cent) and in the neonate (sixty-seven per cent) and declines to about twenty-five per cent in later childhood. The REM state also occurs in mammals. As soon as I turned my attention to dreams I realised the attraction of a theory of dreaming that could integrate the evidence for how the REM state develops in the womb and postnatally in humans (the ontogenetic data) and the evidence for how the REM state evolves in mammals as a whole (the phylogenetic data). Such an explanation is the 'activation-synthesis theory', developed by Hobson and McCarley, already mentioned. Their theory, however, sees dreaming as essentially a meaningless phenomenon resulting from a synthesis of endogenous, random brain stimulation. It cannot, therefore, provide the kind of psychological and biological integration that Hudson is looking for.

An explanation of dreaming that combined the developmental, cross species phylogenetic and psychological perspectives without invalidating the richness of the psychological data, would be a very powerful theory.

The holistic, psychobiological approach presented to you in this book develops three specific and interrelated hypotheses. Together they explain the origin, meaning and function of dreams, and their relationship to the REM state, by integrating data from both the biological and psychological fields.

The first hypothesis deals with the origin and meaning of dreams and arose from the results of my own experiments on dreams. It states that dreams are the sensory analogue (parallel experiences) of emotionally arousing introspections, usually worries or rumination over problems, that are left unresolved when you go to sleep.

The second hypothesis relates to the function of dreams and follows from the first hypothesis. This states that, by giving sensory expression to these emotionally arousing introspections, dreams deactivate the emotional charge created in the autonomic nervous system by the introspections. This frees the resources of the cortex and limbic system to deal with the emotionally arousing contingencies of the next day – after you wake up.

The third hypothesis explains why dreams are expressed in the form of sensory analogues. The answer to this question is found in the biology of dreaming and the REM state itself. Research indicates that genetic information may be programmed during the REM state in the foetus and the neonate. The evidence suggests that the REM state, which is closely associated with dreaming, evolved to programme instinctive behaviour in the foetus and neonate. Such programming of genetically anticipated knowledge would be, necessarily, in the form of incomplete schemata for which analogous sensory components must be identified. (We can see this process beautifully when a baby will seek out and suck on anything analogous to a nipple.) The process gives us the necessary space and flexibility to learn from and adapt to all the ambiguous stimuli in the world, rather than just react to it all. It follows that a prime directive of information processing in the REM state is to search for sensory analogues for these incomplete schemata. Unlike our genetically anticipated knowledge, our waking introspections include already identified sensory components.

We could therefore expect that, if schemata from waking are released during REM sleep, they, too, would be processed in the form of sensory analogues. Our third hypothesis is, therefore, that dreams are expressed as sensory analogues because data processing in the REM state evolved to seek sensory analogues for its completion.

I have derived the evidence in support of these three hypotheses from four main sources:

- the biological studies of dreaming carried out in recent decades,
- my own dreams and the corresponding waking introspections of which they are sensory analogues,
- other peoples' dreams including the analysis of a famous dream of Freud's and Jung which demonstrates their analogical identity to their known waking concerns,
- the work of Silberer (1909,1951) on the 'autosymbolic effect' which demonstrated the existence of an analogue process that converts introspections from waking into sensory dream analogues.

Research on the relationship between dreams, creativity, problem solving, hypnosis and psychotherapy is also considered and, for the first time, a unified theory of consciousness, dreams and the hypnotic state is presented.

I believe the synthesis that Hudson looked forward to is no longer "hovering in mid-distance", you are holding it in your hands.

Our dreams are tales...

Walter de la Mare

Chapter 2

A THOUSAND AND ONE NIGHTS

Theory and experiment

EVERY NIGHT when we dream, we enter a world of magic where the rules of physics, propriety and logic no longer reign: a world where one night we can dine with royalty, converse with famous poets or sportsmen, or walk naked down the street and, on another, we might have the ability to fly or talk with animals. Dreams inhabit a mysterious world where experiences range from the prosaic to the wondrous, from blind terror to sweet delights. Hardly surprising then that from the earliest times humankind has had its theories to explain the happenings in this strange world. Hardly surprising either that dreams were thought to be inhabited by gods and devils.

In the Bible there are many examples of God advising people by means of dreams. Perhaps the most famous example is Pharaoh's dream of seven fat cows followed by seven lean cows, which Joseph interpreted as seven years of plenty followed by seven years of famine. The ancient Greeks believed that the gods communicated the future through dreams. They recognised that not all dreams came true, and thought that true dreams came from the 'Gate of Horn' and false dreams from the 'Gate of Ivory'. Later, temples were erected throughout Greece to encourage, under the guidance of a special priesthood, 'healing dreams' which would indicate what medicine or treatment was appropriate for the dreamer's ailment. Hippocrates placed great emphasis upon symbolism in dreams which he thought indicated particular ailments; for example, dreaming of over-flowing rivers meant an excess of blood.

But Aristotle rejected notions of the divine origin of dreams. How could it be so, he reasoned, since animals also dream. He saw dreams as residual sensory impressions left from waking experience. Plato noted that our higher reasoning faculties were absent in dreams leaving the way open to the expression of unbridled passion. He asserted that in all people there was a lawless wild beast whose presence is glimpsed in dreams of passion and anger. He also thought it possible to have morally superior dreams when reasoning is appropriately stimulated.

The most comprehensive work on dreams to come to us from the ancient times are the five books of dream interpretation written by Artemidorus who lived in Italy in the second century. He held a sophisticated view of dream interpretation believing that the same dream could have a different meaning depending on the character and circumstances of the individual dreamer.

Dreams played a major role in Islamic cultures. The Koran is said to have been largely revealed to Mohammed in a series of dream visions, each one of which appeared to him "like the break of dawn". And records show that he frequently interpreted the dreams of his disciples. Following the example of Mohammed dream interpretation became a widespread feature of Islamic culture. An Arabian dream book of the eleventh century makes mention of several thousand dream interpreters operating at that time. (De Becker, 1968)

The great Arab historian, statesman and Sufi, Ibn Khaldûn, in his 1377 introduction to his monumental history of the world, *The Muqaddimah,* described three types of dream. There are 'clean' dream visions that come from God, allegorical dream visions that are inspired by 'angels' (higher human faculties of perception according to Sufis) and confused dreams which are inspired by

'Satan' (the material world). He noted that, "when the spirit withdraws from the external senses during sleep, it can activate forms from memory which can then become clothed by the imagination in the form of sensory images." He also described a technique for inducing spiritual dreams which involved focusing a clear desire to have such dreams and the repetition of certain phrases indicative of the "perfection of human nature", before falling asleep. He pointed out that this technique could only create a state of preparedness for such dream visions but that it provided no guarantee of receiving them.

Whilst Khaldûn was writing within the accepted religious orthodoxy of his day, this approach does hint at a sophisticated use of the potential of the dream state. From the research evidence explored later in this book, in the section on creativity and dreams, it will become clear that the technique which Khaldûn describes would certainly facilitate the expression of a solution to, or knowledge of, a problem arrived at unconsciously.

Back in Europe, however, during the Middle Ages, studying dreams fell into disrepute and was progressively identified with the devil and sources of temptation.

A more scientific approach to dreams did not become evident until the nineteenth century. Writers such as Maury (1853) and Strumpell (1877) emphasised the role of somatic stimuli, waking experiences and emotions insufficiently inhibited during sleep, in instigating dreams. The idea of the unconscious had also received wide circulation by this time. It was to take Freud, however, to pull these ideas together and combine them with his theory of neurosis to provide a systematic theory of dreaming.

Freud's theory

Freud's theory of dreams was patterned on his theory of neurosis. He saw our neurotic symptoms as the solution to a conflict between a conscious wish and an unconscious repressed wish which would inhibit sleep. Each neurotic symptom was, he believed, an attempt at simultaneously satisfying both wishes.

Freud found that patients often talked about dreams during therapy sessions. He saw the dream as the product of a conflict between the wish to sleep and an unconscious repressed wish from early childhood. During waking, these repressed wishes are active in the unconscious but are held in check or restrained from entering consciousness by the "censor". During sleep, however, this censor is not as alert as it is during waking. Repressed wishes can sometimes get past it, if sufficiently disguised, and be expressed in a dream. Dreams are seen as very similar to neurotic symptoms. The dream according to Freud is the guardian of sleep and it performs this protective role by allowing the expression of an unconscious wish that would otherwise disturb sleep.

He believed that the fact that we wake from a nightmare is the result of the failure of a particular dream to sufficiently disguise the unconscious wishes being expressed, and, as a consequence, the censor is suddenly aroused to full waking alertness. Freud saw the disguise which the unconscious wish wears in the dream as the product of the dream work. This work involves condensation, so that a particular element of the manifest content represents several dream thoughts. It may involve displacement – a dream element whose manifest significance is far less than the disguised latent significance. It also involves representation – primarily the translation of a thought into visual images. The final process is symbolisation, which involves the replacing of a particular character or action with symbols. This helps to disguise the latent content.

Freud stated that the day's residue of problems, worries, unsatisfied wishes or purely indifferent material, may act as, in his words, the "entrepreneur" for a dream, but that the "psychical capital" which makes the dream possible is invariably a repressed infantile wish contained in the subconscious to which the daytime residue becomes linked. The images from waking experiences that are usually contained in the manifest content of dreams come from a repressed infantile wish that sees an affinity with the waking experience and which uses these images, and others from memory, as a sort of disguise to slip past the half-asleep censor and thereby gain a degree of expression for itself.

To discover the meaning of the dream might well be thought nigh impossible given all this distortion, yet more is to come. The waking mind, according to Freud, gives a secondary revision to the manifest content of the dream in order to give it a logical facade. Freud argued that the real meaning of the dream can be uncovered by free association to each of the elements in the dream. The free association can unravel the dream work and reveal the latent wish or wishes that instigated the dream.

Nowhere in Freud's masterpiece, *The Interpretation of Dreams*, did he actually give an example of an analysed dream showing an infantile wish as its source, although he did elsewhere. For the most part, he seemed to have been satisfied with a repressed wish of recent origin, usually sexual in nature, as the source of a dream.

Jung's theory

Jung was a colleague of Freud who became increasingly disaffected with what he felt to be Freud's doctrinaire approach to the investigation of dreams and neurotic symptoms. He came to believe that, while Freud's free association method of dream interpretation led to the identification of the dreamer's psychological complexes, it none the less led away from the real meaning of the dream. He could not accept that the meaning was hidden or disguised to get past a censor so that it could enter consciousness. For him, the symbols in a dream were the natural form in which the unconscious expressed itself. He saw dreams as the unconscious mind's way of correcting distortions and imbalances in the conscious mind. He also saw the unconscious mind as the repository of the "collective unconscious", which he described as the archaic consciousness of primitive man from which the consciousness of modern man develops – just as our body still conforms to a basic pattern that was typical of primitive mammals. These archaic elements of the unconscious are sometimes expressed in dreams and are then called archetypes. To identify these archetypes, according to Jung, a wide knowledge of ancient myths and legends is necessary.

Although most of Jung's theories did not achieve the degree of acceptance conferred on Freud's theories, it is evident that the increasingly widespread view among dream theorists – that dreams can help our conscious mind come to a more balanced view of our emotional problems – owes more to Jung than Freud.

The problem solving theory of dreams was strongly articulated by French (1954, 1964), with a recent interpersonal conflict the focus of problem solving in the dream. The dream substitutes analogous problems which are more suited to the nonverbal thinking characteristic of sleep. He argues that it is more meaningful to work with a series of dreams rather than single dreams when making interpretations

Hall's cognitive theory of dreams:

In 1953 C S Hall advanced a cognitive theory of dreaming which he saw as an extension of "ego psychology". Dreams, according to this theory, are a continuation of normal thinking processes carried on through the medium of pictures or visual images. His research showed that the subjects of dreams were the personal concerns of the dreamer rather than the great political issues of the day. He was collecting dreams from students during the last days of the war with Japan, when the first atomic bomb was exploded. Yet he noted that this catastrophe did not feature in a single dream. He saw dreams as reflecting the dreamer's self conceptions (self image).

Hall likens the dream to a work of art. The artist expresses his ideas through some medium be it writing, pictures, sculpture, music or dance. The essence of the endeavour is that the artist succeeds in communicating his conceptions by translating them into a perceptible medium. In the dream, according to Hall, the dreamer translates his conceptions about his own personal concerns into pictures and thus makes them perceptible. When a thought is made perceptible, Hall says, it is communicated. Unlike the communications of waking life, which he notes may have an audience of millions, the dream is a private communication with an audience of one. This reminds one of the Talmudic idea of the dream being 'a letter to oneself.'

The interpretation of a person's dreams reveals an honest and undistorted view of the dreamer's self conceptions. Hall suggests that this report is unlikely to be as superficial or distorted as reports collected during waking often prove to be.

Hall developed his theory of dreaming in the context of a wide ranging collection of data and a content analysis of that data. When one reads the dream accounts he collected and compares them with known concerns of the dreamer, it is difficult not to be impressed with Hall's theory. Yet the theory has not received the attention one might feel it deserves. A recent book on dreaming by a leading figure in the field (Hobson, 1988) does not even mention his name.

One reason for this neglect might be that the theory seems incomplete. The idea that dreamers send themselves communications in pictures several times a night, which for the most part are forgotten on waking, seems rather wasteful. And the idea that nature evolved and preserved intricate biological machinery for the purpose of creating works of art to be seen only by one person who then, on most occasions, instantly forgets them, makes little intuitive sense. Yet one cannot deny the strength of Hall's empirical findings.

The more I puzzled over the problem the more I came to see that the strength of Hall's empirical approach was also its weakness. There is a vital part of the dream process that could potentially complete the missing pieces of Hall's theory, but it only becomes available initially *through inspection of one's own dreams and one's own waking concerns* in the manner Hall used so brilliantly for other people's dreams.

Scientific method

There are well established precedents for using one's own dreams in dream research. Both Freud and Jung worked extensively with their own dreams. The method which I used to collect representative samples of my own dreams was also used by Ebbinghaus (1885) in his research on memory. He studied the rate of forgetting of nonsense syllables rehearsed prior to sleeping by waking himself during the night at regular intervals and testing his recall. His methodical approach, and the fact that many of his research findings have stood the test of time, demonstrated clearly that scientific method could be applied successfully to one's own subjective experience. Naturally, of course, research findings based on one's own subjective experiences have to be checked against other people's to validate the universality of their application.

Any theory of dreaming put forward as a result of such research, if it is to conform to the highest scientific tradition, should also be in agreement with the major biological findings of recent decades in this field. One would further hope that the theory would reconcile a more wide-ranging set of findings and variables than existing theories. And the theory should also be able to generate novel predictions that are capable of validation.

The dream theories so far described fall short of meeting these criteria in many respects, as will become clear when you read the dream research findings reviewed in the following pages. The various reductionist biological theories of dreaming put forward in recent years see dreaming as essentially a meaningless epiphenomenon of a biological process. These theories will be critically appraised when we consider the biology of dreaming in the next chapter.

It is, of course, for you to decide if you think the evidence I am presenting to support my analogical theory regarding the origin, meaning and function of dreaming, meet the above scientific criteria.

Experimental background

This research project began when I woke up one morning and then drifted back to sleep and found myself dreaming about a castle:

Dream 1

> I start to climb the castle wall. As I get nearer to the top I notice that stones are coming loose and falling down. I feel myself to be in great danger of serious injury.

I woke up still thinking about the dream and remembered that, just before going back to sleep, I had been thinking about a memory from childhood. In this memory, I was playing ball and the ball bounced over a boundary wall. I ran to climb the wall and get it back but, as I pulled myself up, a stone came loose in my hand and I fell backwards. Unfortunately the stone followed me making a large gash in my forehead that required medical attention.

The dream can be seen as a pictorial representation of part of my earlier thoughts – very much as Hall's research suggests. There were, however, some significant changes made in the dream images. The boundary wall, which in reality was just a few feet high, was changed in the dream to a castle wall. The single stone that had come away in my hand was changed in the dream to the entire castle wall beginning to collapse. Perhaps these changes were nothing more than artistic licence since Hall compares dreaming to a form of artistic expression. But my dream did not seem to be a reflection of a specific ongoing problem but a translation of my waking thought pattern into an alternate set of images. My curiosity was aroused. There and then I resolved to collect more of my dreams and compare them with waking concerns to see if this pattern held good across a series of dreams.

To begin with I recorded my dreams whenever I woke up. I found, as have so many before me, that it is essential to make a record of the dream story immediately on awakening, no matter how memorable the dream may appear to be. Otherwise, within a short space of time, it is forgotten. It took some time to acquire the ability to do this consistently, but, eventually, I became so proficient that I would frequently wake up immediately following a dream sequence and could record it there and then.

It proved, however, much more difficult to recall and reflect on my thoughts and experiences of the previous day. I needed to do this, of course, to see if the dream was a reflection of yesterday's waking concerns. The dream is the more recent experience, rich in sensory impressions and emotional content, and at first it can seem difficult to find any significant correspondence with half-forgotten waking experiences of the day before.

I found that the best way to find these correspondences was to rewrite clearly the scribbled dream accounts that had, so often, been hastily written during the night.

Neatly writing or typing my scribbled account of the dream helped to fix it in my memory. I would then bring it back to mind a number of times during the course of the day. Almost invariably a memory of my previous day's experiences would spring to mind which showed an overwhelmingly structural and symbolic correspondence with the events of the dream.

Over the following nine months I continued to collect both my own and other people's dreams and worked at identifying the corresponding waking experiences of the previous day. This clearly indicated that dreams were not simply a continuation of waking thoughts expressed pictorially. Dreams appeared to be concerned with the most emotionally arousing experiences of the previous waking period. These concerns were expressed in symbolic or metaphorical imagery.

The following dream, told to me by someone who had come to me for psychotherapeutic support, perfectly illustrates the process.

This dreamer had recently started a new job involving a training period with other new recruits. He had also been experiencing a degree of anxiety in his social encounters in the period before taking up his new job. One of the things which caused him anxiety was a sudden, almost uncontrollable, desire to laugh at inappropriate moments in company. His inclination to laugh usually occurred when someone spoke intensely or emphatically. To relieve this desire to laugh he had learnt to make a semi-jocose remark and then laugh at his own joke himself. However, in his new job, one or two people had not responded well to this behaviour. When he told me about this problem, I ventured the opinion that perhaps his desire to laugh was due less to his perception of humour in the situation and more to an effort to relieve the anxiety generated in himself by seeing the tension he was creating in the other person. A couple of days later he reported this dream to me:

Dream 2

> I am in church and I want to go up to read the gospel but people keep getting in my way. Suddenly Terry Wogan is standing on the altar. The church has a wall dividing the altar from the main body of the church where the audience is seated. Now I am at the other side of this wall and I am urinating. Terry Wogan can see what I am doing (but no one else can) and is laughing at me. The people in the church assume I have cracked a joke and all start laughing."

The correspondence between the subject's waking experience and the dream is fairly self-evident. Terry Wogan standing beside him stands for the public image other people have of him. He thinks people see him as a witty personality like the television star, Terry Wogan, whom he had recently seen in person and who shares his Irish nationality. People, therefore, regarding him as a witty personality, assume he cracked a joke when he laughs, but he's really laughing at his own embarrassment. Note the connection with the common vulgar expressions 'pissing myself ' to denote a state of tension and the phrase 'pissing myself laughing' to denote a state of uncontrollable laughing.

The church setting is also appropriate because this person saw himself as religious with a responsibility to promote 'the gospel'. His problem relating to people is making it difficult for him to fulfil that responsibility. This is symbolically expressed in the opening sequence of the dream when he tries to go up to the altar to read the gospel but people keep getting in his way. The barrier in the dream between himself and the people who can see Terry Wogan laughing, but not him urinating, can be seen as an analogy for the dichotomy of himself as other people see him in company – 'laughing' – and as he really is – 'pissing himself'.

The dream can be seen as a metaphorical expression of the dreamer's waking anxiety from the perspective that I had put to him. Thus this dream would appear to confirm Hall's theory that dreams express the dreamer's self conceptions. The dream does, as Hall says, convert the dreamer's concepts into perceptions and, in so doing, the dreamer succeeds in communicating his ideas very much as the artist can be said to have communicated his ideas when the work of art is created. But surely dreams, however aesthetically pleasing, must serve some adaptive function for the organism?

The most surprising finding from my research, so far, was that the dream *always* gave metaphorical or symbolical expression to waking concerns. This applied not just to concepts but to people as well. For example, a husband who was seen as behaving in a dominating manner was replaced in a dream by a forceful school master known to the dreamer.

At this point in my exploratory research, having decoded several dozen of my own and other people's dreams, it seemed time to adopt a more systematic approach to dream collection. This was because I could not yet claim that the dreams I had collected and decoded were representative of dreaming as a whole. It could be argued that the dreams that spontaneously cross the threshold into waking consciousness are in some way more memorable or more coherent than the average unremembered dream.

I knew from reviewing the experimental dream research of recent decades (see the next chapter) that dreaming is strongly associated with a state of active brain arousal, occurring about every ninety minutes during sleep, and referred to as 'rapid eye movement sleep' or REM sleep. The REM periods tend to be shorter at the beginning of the night and to get longer as the night progresses. I decided to set my alarm clock for two hours earlier than normal and immediately record any dreams I could recall at that time. When the alarm went off, I immediately wrote down any dreams I could recall. Often a dream would be easily recalled but, equally often, only a vague memory of dreaming would come to mind. When that happened I discovered, to my surprise, that the act of writing down the few details of the dream that I could still remember would serve to bring back a clear memory of further dream material.

Whilst doing this I also continued to record any dreams I could remember on normal awakening. I found that it was important to record *all* dreams, irrespective of how irrelevant or even nonsensical they might appear at the time of recall. Later, those apparently meaningless image sequences made perfect sense when I identified the waking experience to which they related. On some mornings I recorded up to five dreams, on others only two, in which case several themes might be recorded within a dream and the dream sequence would consequently be unusually long. I maintained this method of dream collection for three weeks.

This study found that the subject matter of the recorded dreams, as expected, related to my waking concerns. It also supported my previous finding that dreams are not simply a visual expression of personal concerns but are a metaphorical visual translation of those waking concerns.

That dreams use metaphor has been noted by many theorists but that *all* dreams use metaphor is a new finding. My research indicates that, not only do all dreams use metaphor, but that the entire dream sequence is a metaphorical expression of a waking concern. This means that everybody and everything in the dream sequence is an analogous substitute for some person, thing or event in waking life. In other words, the plot, or theme, set out while you are awake is preserved in the dream but the locations, props and the entire cast is replaced. The dreamer is aware of himself in the dream because that is awareness not perception, but where the dreamer has been objectifying his own identity, or part of it, then that identity is represented by someone else in the dream. We saw an example of this in the second dream where the part of the dreamer's persona was played by Terry Wogan.

We are not seeing metaphor used as a dramatic device to highlight certain principles or concepts, as might be used in the creation of a work of art, but rather the translation of the waking concern into an analogous sensory scenario. The next dream illustrates the process:

Dream 3

Scene I

> I got my hair cut in a new style that had spiky hair sticking up in the air. A man passes me by as I walk down the road. He sticks his hand out in the manner of a referee at a football match and calls out, "that hair style doesn't suit you". I feel crestfallen and I immediately flatten my hair.

Scene II

> I have put on a new Harris tweed suit. It looks very good except that it has a kind of skirt wrapped around the trousers. I feel a bit embarrassed about this feature. I detach the skirt and look in the mirror and think to myself that it looks okay now.

The previous day I had bought two sweatshirts in a street market without the facilities to try them on. Thinking about my purchase on the way home, I reflected that one of the sweatshirts might look too young on me because of the two white bands across the body which made it look rather like a football shirt. I decided that it would definitely not suit me and I would have to get rid of it.

These thoughts are expressed in the dream by means of their translation into an analogical sensory scenario. In the dream, the unsuitable 'too young' style of sweatshirt is replaced by a new style of haircut. I had recently seen a young man get this new style while waiting my turn at the hairdresser's. This image expresses my expectation that the sweatshirt would be more suited to a younger person. The person sticking his hand out like a referee and telling me that the hairstyle was unsuitable expresses my feeling that the sweatshirt was unsuitable. By behaving like a referee in a football match he makes a visual reference to my waking thought that the sweatshirt looks like a football shirt. By flattening my hair I get rid of the hairstyle just as in waking life I had resolved to get rid of the sweatshirt.

Scene two in the dream relates to my purchase of the second sweatshirt. I had hesitated to buy it because the pastel colour seemed to me to be a shade more usually worn by women. On further reflection I rejected this sexist attitude and decided that, if I liked it, I would buy it. On the way home, I reflected that, unlike the other sweatshirt, this one would suit me. Later that evening, by chance, I saw a TV programme about the island of Harris and the manufacture of Harris tweed. The programme concluded with a display of Harris tweed suits, the style of which I thought unorthodox although I liked the fabric. We can clearly see that the analogy used in the dream came from the TV programme. Interestingly Freud maintained that part of the *manifest* content of the dream came from the waking experience of the previous day, which in the case of this dream can be seen to be true. But what my research shows is that the *latent* content of a dream also comes from the experience of the previous day.

The Harris tweed suit stands for the second sweatshirt as will become clear. The skirt wrapped around the trousers is an analogy for my sexist views concerning the colour. My removing of the skirt is analogous to me discarding my sexist views concerning the colour. My expectation that the sweatshirt would look all right is made manifest in the dream when I look in the mirror and note that the suit looks well on me, now the skirt is discarded. There is also a pun in the analogy of suit for the sweatshirt because this is the sweatshirt that I anticipated would 'suit' me.

We can see, therefore, that the two dreams represent, in an analogical sensory form, my thoughts and feelings concerning the purchase of two sweatshirts.

Up to this point, my findings indicate that dreams represent our waking concerns expressed in an analogical sensory format. If this hypothesis is correct then, in principle, it ought to be possible to predict one's own dreams from an inspection of one's own waking concerns. In practice, of course, there are a number of difficulties attendant on such an experiment. For example, would it be possible to maintain the continuous self monitoring that identifying likely waking concerns would require? And would this process of self monitoring and prediction affect the dream process? A further problem is the necessity of devising a means of collecting the night's dreams.

Notwithstanding these potential difficulties, I resolved to carry out the experiment.

In order to get as complete a collection of the night's dreams as possible, I woke myself up every two hours with an alarm clock and recorded whatever dreams I could remember. The predicted themes, based on a reflection of the concerns that had occupied my attention during the day, were written down prior to going to sleep. The first time I tried this I had, by the next morning, recorded three dreams.

The first dream theme related to a domestic incident of the previous day, which was one of the predicted sources of dream material. It was an accurate symbolic representation of my perception and emotional reaction to the incident. The next two dream sequences portrayed different aspects of a predicted theme which related to my reflections concerning the analogical theory of dreams. I had been rereading my notes on the previous year's research on dreams which included a summary of existing dream theories. I again noticed how Freud had mentioned that the previous day's experiences were reflected in the manifest content of the dream. Freud referred to this as the "day's residue". I noticed how, in my own collection of dreams, there was usually an item or two in the manifest content of the dream that was related to the previous day's experiences. It would appear, however, that Freud had not observed that the latent content was also a reflection of the previous day's experiences.

I reflected that Jung's concept of the 'shadow' may have derived from observing the self as object metaphorically expressed in dreams, as in the Terry Wogan character in dream 3. I further noticed that other dream researchers were also investigating dreaming from the perspective of finding the adaptive significance of dreams. The 'sentinel hypothesis', put forward by Snyder in 1966, sees sleep as putting the animal at risk from predators. He suggested that the periodic activation of the brain by the REM state, followed by a brief awakening, may leave animals better prepared to deal with danger. But the problem with this idea is that, even if such an adaptation has taken place, it can scarcely account for the complexity and meta-phorical nature of human dreaming. In 1959, Ullman put forward similar thoughts with regard to human dreaming. He saw dreaming as possibly preparing humans for the kind of reality they are likely to encounter on awakening. But this hypothesis was incompatible with the evidence about dreaming that I was gathering.

One of my major waking preoccupations that day, therefore, was a consideration of the work of other theorists and my search for points of similarity that existed between their work and mine. I had wondered if it would be necessary, when I eventually reported on my research, to detail these points of correspondence. That evening, as I reviewed the day's activities to make my dream predictions, it seemed likely to me that my preoccupation with studying other dream theories during the day might well become a theme that featured in my dreams that night. As expected, one of my dreams that night did indeed reflect that theme. This is that dream:

Dream 4

Scene I

> We are searching for buried treasure under a pile of bricks in a field. I'm wondering will we divide the treasure between us or is it a case of 'finders keepers'.

Scene II

> Then it seems we are back in time, a time shortly after a Christ-like figure has lived. Now we are digging a well. We have a bottle of water with us. Someone finishes the bottle off. I am aware that everything will be all right because the well will be full in twelve hours.

The first scene of the dream obviously relates to my reading of other people's theories and wondering whether I should point out the parallels with certain aspects of my own ideas on dreams. The symbol of the buried treasure is appropriate for the search for the meaning of dreams, given that I place a high value on such research.

The Christ-like figure in the second scene refers to Freud whose photograph has always brought biblical associations to my mind. The pile of bricks relates to the present state of Freud's dream theory as I see it – collapsed in ruins.

The well is a symbol for creativity and the specific creativity involved in the discovery of the meaning of dreams. This is an appropriate symbol, not only because one has to dig under the ground to find water and one also has to dig, as it were, under the manifest content of the dream to find the latent content, but also because a well had recently come to my attention as a symbol of creativity in Chinese literature.

The bottle of water present during our digging refers to the parallels between other theorists' work and my own. A bottle of water is a small amount compared to a full well of water. The parallels between other theorist's work and my own represent small discoveries about the dream process. In the dream, I don't mind who drinks the bottle of water. That is to say, I don't mind who gets the credit for these discoveries. The well will be full in twelve hours means that in twelve hours I will have my night's collection of dreams which I expect to be full of creative insights.

The final dream relates to the experiment itself:

Dream 5

> We are looking for buried eggs. There is a hen nearby. Someone finds a single egg buried near the hen. This egg was very close to the surface. I say: "It's an old egg – probably been there for days – but there's still a whole pile of eggs buried somewhere".

The hen represents the REM state or dream generator. The egg that was found only lightly buried near the surface relates to the manifest content of the dream. It is found near the hen, lightly buried, meaning that it is easily identified with the dreamer's waking experience. This relates to those aspects of the manifest content, which Freud had observed relate to the dreamer's waking experience of the previous day. The egg appears to me to be old because the observation about the manifest content was made by Freud many years ago. The pile of eggs that I am looking for refers to the dream themes identified the night before which I expect to find buried in my night's dreams. Chickens develop from the genetic code hidden in the egg and in a very real sense dreams can be decoded to show that they are a translation of specific information from the past into a new sensory structure.

This dream can be seen as a clear metaphorical expression of my hopes and reflections of the day before concerning the dream experiment that I was planning. The dream is not a wish fulfilment, as might be expected from Freudian theory. It doesn't show me finding the eggs, rather it expresses my expectation that the dream themes will be found 'buried' in the night's dreams. We can see clearly that the dream does not go beyond the waking thought in another medium as Hall's theory might lead one to expect. Like the other dreams that have been analysed it is the translation of waking experience into a sensory metaphorical analogue.

My results were therefore supportive of the hypothesis I was testing. Two of the three recorded dreams related to predicted themes. One dream related to the experiment itself. On the other hand I had predicted five dream themes, three of which failed to manifest as recorded dreams. This might be because I failed to record the relevant dreams. It could also be because they didn't result in dreams.

I continued the experiment for another four nights and successfully predicted two or three dream themes each night. As the experiment progressed I recalled a far greater number of dreams and it became clear that, whilst I could predict some dream themes, unpredicted themes also featured in dreams. Whilst these were metaphorical representations of waking concerns it was by no means clear to me why they should have been chosen as dream themes in preference to my predicted themes. At this point a further complication emerged. Even when a predicted theme featured in a dream, I had not usually predicted the particular aspect of the waking concern that was featured. My predicted dream themes tended to be fairly general whilst their expression in a dream was much more specific.

At the conclusion of the experiment, I had mixed results. On the one hand they convincingly supported the hypothesis that dreams were metaphorical expressions of waking concerns but, on the other, the basis on which those waking concerns were chosen as the subject matter of my dreams was unclear.

I had assumed that the most pressing waking concerns would form the subject matter of dreams and, indeed, had used that as the criterion on which to base my predictions of what waking concerns would form the basis of dreams. Some of the dreams from the experiment showed that was not the case. Not only did less important waking concerns become the subject matter of dreams but a major concern which I had expected to form the subject matter of at least one dream did not feature at all in an extensive night's collection of dreams. It seemed likely that, if the basis on which waking experiences were selected to form the subject matter of dreams could be identified, this might provide a significant clue as to why we dreamed.

Over the next twelve months I continued to collect and decipher my own dreams and those offered to me by other people in the hope of finding some criterion that would identify the basis on which waking experiences became the subject matter of dreams. Although the many dreams I collected and decoded over this period continued to provide evidence that dreams are sensory analogues of waking experiences, no clue emerged as to what selection criterion was being used. The fact that some of our dream predictions, based on the perceived importance of the waking concern, successfully predicted dream themes shows that the perceived importance of the concern may be one of the criteria. But there must be some modifying factor also involved.

29

As I puzzled over this I decided to write up my research findings to date. Whilst doing so I made an exciting discovery. The significance of a predicted dream theme *that failed to materialise as a dream* suddenly became apparent.

This is what happened as I tried to predict my dreams. As I read over and wrote up my notes I saw that, by the third day of the experiment, I was finding the whole process extremely stressful. The increasing tiredness, together with the effort of constant reflection on the previous night's dreams, were taking their toll. I found myself getting increasingly short-tempered and irritable. The experiment was also proving stressful for my wife whose sleep was being disturbed by the alarm every two hours to wake me up and by me turning the light on to record the dreams. This stress bomb finally exploded on the third night as we were about to go to bed. We had a row. When I finally got into bed, having given full vent to my frustrations, I reflected that this heated exchange with my wife, in which I (temporarily) perceived her to have changed from a supportive ally to a hostile and unsympathetic critic of my research, must surely form the basis of a dream. Before turning out the light I hastily added this theme to my list of dream predictions.

The next day, however, it was clear that the 'row' was in no way reflected in the night's dream experiences I recorded. It may well have been that I failed to record the dream in which this theme was expressed. However, I had recorded five dream sequences from that night and I could not help contrasting the failure of this theme to manifest itself with the number of times the theme of the experiment itself was featured during the first night's dreams. Was there some significant way in which these two waking concerns differed that might account for the reason why one was apparently repeatedly selected to have various aspects of it explored in a dream whilst the other was apparently ignored?

Yes, there was.

During the row with my wife, *I had discharged my feelings straight away.* In contrast, the feelings aroused by the prospect of the experiment were *not* discharged. (I am using the term 'feeling' here in the sense of a drive towards, or away from, experiencing a particular sequence of stimuli.) Because the highly aroused feelings relating to an event in the future – the prospect of the experiment – were not discharged in the present, I searched for the buried treasure in my dream, I searched for the buried eggs, I dug the well.

A previous argument with my wife that did become the subject matter of a dream came back to mind:

Dream 6

I'm wearing punk-type coloured spectacles which I refuse to change, since I have already paid for them. I'm aware that my wife is telling her mother that I'm unwilling to change them.

This dream is based on my experience prior to going to sleep. Following a disagreement with my wife, I saw myself as the injured party. My wife indicated that she was willing to forget the incident. Perceiving myself as the injured party, 'having paid the price' of being mistreated, I feel unwilling to change my aggressive perspective. This is metaphorically represented in the dream as my unwillingness to change my 'punk spectacles'. I reflected that my wife must see me as unwilling to make-up and forget about the issue. I reflected to myself that *I* was the injured party and therefore entitled to my viewpoint – 'I *had* paid the price'.

My wife's mother appears in the dream sequence as a stand in for my wife's objective self telling *her* subjective self that I am unwilling to change my perspective, just as I had imagined her doing before I went to sleep. Clearly in this scene, unlike in the previous disagreement, I had not yet expressed my feelings and views on the situation.

I have already noted that everybody and everything perceived in a dream is a metaphorical or analogical replacement for somebody or thing from waking. Yet my wife's identity doesn't change in the dream. Why? The reason is that I don't actually see her. But I *am* aware of what she is doing. I know she is close by but I don't actually perceive her in the dream. Her objective self, the self I had imagined her talking to, is analogically represented in the dream by her mother with whom she enjoys a close relationship. This dream is, therefore, a metaphorical acting out of my introspected but unexpressed views and emotions concerning a disagreement with my wife.

The experience that resulted in a dream was one that involved the arousal of feelings which were not acted out or given expression. This then was the qualifying criterion that I had been searching for. My previous research had indicated that dreams were a metaphorical reflection of emotionally arousing concerns of the previous day. This led me to the question: what criterion or rule was used to select between those emotionally arousing concerns, the specific dream themes I had, hitherto, been unable to identify? The answer was now clear. What becomes the subject matter of dreams is not our emotionally arousing concerns per se but our unexpressed emotionally arousing views about those concerns. The new hypothesis can be stated as follows: Dreams are a sensory analogue of emotionally arousing introspections (which I term 'activated drive schemata') *not* manifested or acted out during waking.

My analogy hypothesis has in common with Freud's

theory the idea that dreams have a latent meaning. It differs from Freud's theory, however, in two ways:

1 The origin of the dream lies in conscious introspections and not in 'subconscious infantile impulses';

2 Dreams are not disguised or distorted wishes, they are sensory analogues of unexpressed emotionally arousing introspections from waking.

My hypothesis has in common with Hall's cognitive theory the suggestion that dreams relate to the conscious emotional concerns of the dreamer. Unlike Hall's theory, which sees the dream as a continuation of waking thought in another medium, my hypothesis specifically states that the dream is a replay of certain previous emotionally arousing thoughts from waking. It also differs from Hall's theory in that it specifically predicts that *all* dreams are expressed in the form of a sensory analogue.

When I reviewed all the dreams I had collected, and the waking experiences on which they were based, they all proved compatible with this new hypothesis. For example, if you consider dream number 3 (page 22), in which I purchased two sweaters in a street market without facilities to try them on, you can clearly see that the resultant dream sequences were metaphorical translations of my anticipated reactions to how the sweatshirts would look when I tried them on. In this instance the introspections were anticipating my future reactions to trying on the sweatshirts. These anticipated reactions did not take place because when I tried the sweatshirts on they were too small and I gave them to my wife. Thus the anticipated reactions did not take place at all during waking. They were, however, expressed in the form of a sensory analogue in the dream.

I continued collecting my own and other people's dreams over the next several years. Gradually I identified a number of reasons why the emotionally arousing introspections that result in dreams do not become manifest during waking. These include the fact that the anticipated experience may still be in the future at the time of going to sleep. Another reason is that the dreamer, before falling asleep, might have been introspecting about emotionally arousing events from the past that could not manifest in the present. A further reason is that the dreamer, when awake, may have wrongly anticipated how certain events would turn out. I also found that dreams can result from introspections about emotionally involving television programmes. In the chapter on the psychology of dreaming I will give examples of dreams resulting from these types of experiences.

What, then, is the function of dreams? The research reported in this book suggests that dreams involve emotionally arousing introspections translated into sensory analogues. The dreamer acts out his introspected scenario from waking in the form of a sensory analogue. I hypothesise that this deactivates the emotionally arousing introspection from waking. The dream, by releasing these programmes of activation, frees the resources of the cortex and limbic system to attend to the emotionally arousing contingencies of the next waking period.

I am therefore putting forward two hypotheses:

Hypothesis 1

Dreams are a sensory analogue of emotionally arousing introspections (activated drive schemata) which are still active at sleep onset.

Hypothesis 2

The expression of these activated drive schemata as a sensory analogue deactivates them thus releasing the cortex and limbic system from having to maintain a readiness to respond to stimuli associated with these programmes of activation.

This second hypothesis raises an important question. Why does the brain convert the emotionally arousing introspections into a sensory analogue?

I felt sure the answer could be found by reviewing the major findings of the research into the biology of dreaming. When I did this I found that, not only is dreaming expressed in the form of a sensory analogue, but that it could be expected to be expressed in this way.

As I carried out my review of the biological research, set out in the next and subsequent chapters, my approach was consistent with the advice of Farr (1993) when discussing the scientific method: "Once you have the right theory though, it can be used to reinterpret what is already known... It is not so much new evidence as new thinking that is called for... It is foolish to ignore what we already know from experimental research."

It is my aim in this book, therefore, not only to introduce new data in support of the analogical mind hypotheses put forward, but also to demonstrate the wide support for these hypotheses that can be found from existing experimental research.

Sleep that knits up
    the ravelled sleeve of care,
the death of each day's life,
    sore labour's bath,
balm of hurt minds,
    great nature's second course,
chief nourisher in life's feast.

William Shakespeare

Chapter 3

THE SLEEPING MIND

The biology of dreaming

IN THE LAST forty five years, sleep research has turned into a major scientific enterprise and a wealth of new biological data has emerged. A major stimulus to research in this area was Aserinsky & Kleitman's finding (1953) of a regular change in a sleeping subject's electroencephalogram (EEG) reading. These are recordings of the electrical brain patterns made by means of electrodes placed on the skull. Their research showed that sleep consisted of two discrete phases which alternated periodically throughout the night, rather than the continuum which had previously been assumed. One phase which occurred about every ninety minutes was accompanied by rapid eye movements and for that reason was called REM sleep.

A more detailed study by Dement and Kleitman in 1957 confirmed that REM sleep occurred about every ninety

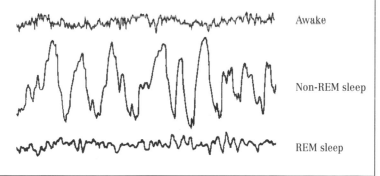

Electroencephalogram (EEG) recordings

When two electrodes are placed on the scalp and connected to an amplifier/ recorder (the EEG machine) the voltage between the two can be recorded continuously on paper. The results below clearly show the similarity between the brain waves in waking state and REM sleep where most dreaming occurs.

Awake

Non-REM sleep

REM sleep

minutes and occupied, on average, one and a half to two hours of total sleep time. Subjects awakened from REM sleep were able to recall a dream on eighty per cent of occasions whereas subjects awakened from non-REM sleep, later to be called slow wave sleep (SWS), were only able to recall a dream on around seven per cent of occasions. It was suggested that the small percentage of dreams recalled from SWS might represent memories of dreams persisting from earlier REM phases. They also noted that recordings from SWS could be further divided into four stages (I-IV) according to progressive changes in the slow wave pattern.

The relationship between dreaming and non-REM sleep, however, is not as clear cut as Dement and Kleitman's 1957 paper suggests. Dreaming *does* occur outside REM sleep. In fact about sixty per cent of non-REM awakenings result in reports of mental activity of some sort. More often than not, as Foulkes showed in his research published in 1985, these reports have the characteristic of a dream fragment, if not a dream scenario. At other times, thinking seems to be repetitive, going over the same ground, not getting anywhere. Foulkes suggested that non-REM dreaming may often reveal a breakdown in the same processes that serve fluent dreaming in REM sleep. The processes of dream formation in non-REM sleep may show, therefore, a lesser engagement of the dream production system that operates at full flow during REM sleep proper.

Some research on dreaming cats carried out by Jouvet and Michel (1959) identified a further indication of REM sleep. They noted that the state was also accompanied by an inhibition of antigravity muscles – tonic immobility. It soon became apparent that the REM state was characteristic not only of humans but also of nearly all viviparous mammals. It has even been found in birds, though lasting only for brief periods of time. The internationally agreed system for recording sleep phases now comprises the recording of signals coming from the muscles by electromyograph (EMG), together with the recording of eye movements by electro-oculograph (EOG) and, of course, brain waves by EEG.

It will become clear that electrical signals called PGO spikes play a key role in both the generation of the REM state and also in dreams themselves. These signals arise in and progress through three areas of the brain. They start in the pons (the lower brainstem) and travel up via a part of the midbrain called the geniculate body to the occipital cortex in the higher brain. (Thus the name PGO spikes – ponto-geniculate occipital spikes – from pons, geniculate and occipital.)

An important distinction was made by Mourizzi (1963) when he noted that the REM state could be divided into tonic and phasic components. The tonic component is the underlying passive state where muscles are immobilised. This lasts throughout REM sleep.

PGO spikes

The visual brain stimulates itself in REM sleep through a mechanism reflected in EEG recordings as PGO waves. These signals originate in the pons (P) from the neurones that move the eyes and are then conducted to both the lateral geniculate (G) body in the thalamus and to the occipital cortex (O) - hence PGO spikes.

Occipital cortex

Geniculate

Pons

Periodically superimposed upon this passive state is the phasic component compromising bursts of activity when PGO spikes occur, the eyes dart about, there is fine muscle twitching and breathing patterns and heartrate changes (Hartmann, 1967).

The phasic components are not strictly confined to the REM stage. PGO spikes are observed in the geniculate body prior to REM stage (Dement, 1968). The work of Jouvet (1967) established that tonic and phasic components are based upon different anatomical mechanisms. He showed that, under certain conditions, tonic and phasic components can be separated. The following year Dement concluded that an important principle was suggested by these results, namely that at least two distinct neurological systems were responsible for the REM state: a system that generates the phasic events, particularly PGO spikes, and a system that produces the tonic phenomena, particularly the REM state itself.

The importance of these findings is that they suggest that a number of processes come together during a full blown REM state, which may also occur discretely at other phases of sleep. Thus the similarity in the EEG sleep onset (stage 1) and REM sleep, and the fact that dreams have been recorded from both stages, might mean that there is a similar form of data processing going on in the cortex in both stages. As Foulkes suggests, sleep onset dreaming may well mean a partial engagement of the dream production system at that time, whereas in REM sleep, we see the full engagement of this system.

It was Dement who was responsible for the first systematic studies of REM deprivation in 1960. Using human subjects, who were awakened at the onset of a REM phase, Dement succeeded in curtailing the amount of time they spent in REM sleep. He found that on the recovery night there was a marked increase, compared to baseline, in the amount of time spent in REM sleep. Further studies by Ferguson and Dement, published in 1968, showed that, not only was there an increase in REM sleep time, but also an increase in the frequency of phasic events. Dement found that, sometimes, when an animal (he used a cat) was gently aroused at the onset of a REM period, the REM period could be effectively derailed while allowing a discharge of a large number of PGO spikes. Two days of this procedure was followed by a small or non-existent rebound. These results indicated the crucial factor in REM sleep deprivation – compensation was by phasic events rather than tonic events, ie rather than the REM state per se.

A further important finding reported by Dement was that prolonged REM deprivation in cats brought about an increase in the general level of arousal, especially primitive emotions such as sexual desire and rage. He had expected that the REM deprivation would lead to hallucinations accompanied by the discharge of PGO spikes. However, administration of the drug paca-chlorophenylalanine (PCPA), a compound which inhibits the synthesis of serotonin in the brain, to REM-deprived animals leads, within a few days of being on the drug, to the appearance of PGO spikes when they are awake, hallucinatory behaviour and a markedly accentuated drive state. The animals underwent a profound personality change resulting in hypersexuality, rage behaviour and over-eating. However, as time goes on, the spike discharge becomes evenly dispersed throughout waking and sleeping and the animal becomes very lethargic.

These findings suggested to Dement that there were two systems of drive discharge the discharge of our instinctive impulses – and that there was a finite amount of energy available to do this which could become depleted. The first is during waking by drive-oriented behaviour such as thirst, hunger or sexual urges. The second is by means of PGO spikes. The two systems do not operate at the same time because PGO spikes are not observed in animals when executing drive-oriented behaviour. You do not see PGO spikes when animals are eating, for instance. These results led Dement to conclude that the primary role of REM sleep was to provide a 'safety valve' outlet for the discharge of the drive system.

Dement was not entirely happy with this notion, however, because he wrote elsewhere "it seems naive to suggest that the REMs exist in the adult organism to prevent the nervous system from becoming over-excitable". The major evidence which Dement accumulated to suggest two types of drive discharge system still stands, and we shall see that the function of the second drive discharge system is far more vital and sophisticated than that of a 'safety valve outlet' that he suggested.

Dement was also one of the co-authors (Roffwarg, Muzio and Dement, 1966) of a very different theory of the function of the REM state. This is the so-called 'ontogenetic hypothesis' put forward to explain one of the most surprising discoveries about REM sleep. Research has shown that REM sleep occurs most frequently in the young and decreases as we get older. During the last trimester of pregnancy the foetus spends up to eighty per cent of sleep time in REM sleep. This declines to sixty-seven per cent at birth, declines further to approximately twenty-five per cent later in childhood and stays at approximately this level until old age, when it declines still further. The amount of REM sleep at birth is directly related to the maturity of the animal. Those species born with their brains and physical abilities well developed show little REM sleep. In contrast, species who are born very immature show high levels of REM sleep. A species such as the guinea pig, which is well developed at birth, shows only about fifteen per cent REM sleep, whereas the rat, which is born blind and immobile, shows over ninety-five per cent REM sleep. The rat quickly matures and, within one month, REM sleep has declined to thirty per cent of total sleep time. Dement and his colleagues concluded that the primary role of REM sleep is in the very young and that it may be providing stimulation to the developing cerebrum in the stimulus-poor intrauterine environment. There can be little doubt that any comprehensive theory of REM sleep must be able to explain not only REM sleep in adulthood but also its preponderance during gestation and early childhood.

Dement's idea of two methods of drive discharge has also been used by Vogel (1979) to explain his finding that subjects suffering from endogenous depression showed an improvement in their condition when deprived of REM sleep. For a sustained improvement, REM sleep deprivation has to last for about three weeks. Vogel's argument suggests that these patients may have been discharging too much drive through REM sleep and that, by preventing REM sleep, we are increasing the drive motivation available to the subject when awake. He suggests that, while REM sleep deprivation shows some arousal effects in normal subjects, these effects are not as dramatic as with depressed subjects, because normal subjects are already near the ceiling for excitability. To support this idea, he refers to a well established finding that antidepressant drugs, which suppress REM sleep, have little effect on normal people, yet depressed people can have their drive or motivation lifted by these REM depressing drugs. Vogel concluded that one of the functions of REM sleep is to modulate drive-oriented behaviour so as to permit greater flexibility in the expression of instinctive behaviour in higher organisms.

In other words, to damp down instincts. Whilst I have to agree with Dement that this idea of damping down instincts is rather crude, nonetheless, Vogel's idea – that two methods of drive discharge might be linked to both instinctive behaviour and the required flexibility in the expression of behaviour in higher mammals – will be seen to have some merit.

Activation synthesis theory

The so called 'activation synthesis theory' was first put forward by Hobson and McCarley in 1977 and Hobson developed it further in work published in 1988. They saw dreaming as the result of the cortex's attempt to make sense of the random barrage of signals sent from the lower brain. The dream synthesis that we create may reveal something of how our personality habitually operates, according to the authors of this theory. The random testing of pattern generators may also serve a maintenance and developmental function. It is now quite apparent, as the research of Hobson, McCarley and others shows, that the REM state is controlled by mechanisms in the lower brain. It is also clear that dreaming in the REM state is more intense during bursts of rapid eye movements and other phasic signals.

My evidence seriously questions that dreaming is a result of a synthesis of random signals.

We dream to forget theory

We dream in order to forget, is the idea put forward by Crick and Mitchison in 1983. They suggested that dream sleep may be an unlearning process, a way of removing unwanted or parasitic forms of associations in the neocortex. This may arise during structural growth of the cortex, through modification of the existing associational network, as a result of experience. The stimulation which the cortex receives during REM sleep may excite these parasitic modes, rather than normal patterns of associations which need highly specific signals to stimulate them. A mechanism of reverse learning is then thought to adjust the synapses that underlay these modes so that this pattern of activity is less likely to occur in the future. They suggested that in our dreams we observe these modes being stimulated. Two years later Hudson pointed out that the clear implication of this theory is that people who frequently recall dreams should be more "addled in their wits" than non-recallers, a finding unsupported by research.

The computer theory

The 'computer' theory of dreaming was first introduced by Evans and Newman in 1964 and further expanded by Evans and Evans in 1983. This theory sees REM sleep as programming the brain. During REM sleep, the brain is disconnected from the outside world by inhibition of anti-gravity muscles and sensory input, thus it can be compared to an off-line computer. The brain contains a myriad of programmes which can be updated during this off line time of REM sleep. This proposal has the advantage of seeing the REM state as a positive state with specific accomplishments. It also has the merit of allowing us to see REM sleep in the neonate and young as a time when the 'software' of the brain is programmed.

Jouvet's theory

The computer theory has similarities with the theory put forward by Jouvet in 1978. It was Jouvet who made the discovery of the inhibition of anti-gravity muscles during REM sleep. He suggested that REM sleep might have the role of programming the central nervous system for the purpose of maintaining or organising instinctive behaviour. He argues that the programming of instinctive behaviour on a continuous basis, rather than a once and for all basis, during development would enable a more efficient expression of instinctive behaviour. Since the original programming must interact with the animal's experience, then REM sleep might allow either the original programming to be reasserted (nature over environment) or the effects of the experience to modify the programming (environment over nature). Jouvet has shown that REM sleep is controlled by a very primitive part of the brain and that, when the neocortex is removed, REM sleep still occurs although not slow wave sleep. He also showed that, when a small area of the mid-brain is removed, cats seem to act out their dreams (Jouvet, 1965, 1977). Following this operation, animals during REM sleep indulge in stereotyped behaviour such as chasing or attacking an invisible object, displaying fright behaviour or indulging in grooming or drinking behaviour.

Consistent with Jouvet's theory, is the observation that newborn babies display what appear to be sophisticated expressions of emotions during REM sleep, such as perplexity, disdain, scepticism and mild amusement, which are not observed during waking (Roffwarg, Muzio and Dement, 1966). Young babies smile in REM sleep weeks before social smiling can be observed (Hunt, 1989). It was suggested by Hobson (1989) that, because newborn babies know how to breathe and swallow as soon as they are born, these behaviours are learned in REM sleep. He notes that observation of foetal lambs has shown breathing movements of the chest wall in REM sleep, even though, of course, there is no air to breathe. It's possible that behaviours are being programmed or rehearsed in REM sleep which will only appear later in social life when appropriate sensory analogues are identified. However, Jouvet's theory is less plausible when we consider REM sleep and the older child and adult. No analysis of the dreams from REM sleep has shown a consistent pattern of interaction between waking behaviour and what might be considered rehearsal of instinctive drives or behaviour.

If we leave the mystery of dreaming aside for the moment and consider Dement's and Jouvet's research findings together, a nice integration becomes possible between the role and function of REM sleep in the foetus and the neonate. Dement's research suggests that there is a system of drive discharge in the normal waking system and an alternative system that operates during REM sleep. If we also consider the dominance of REM sleep in the foetus and neonate then drive discharge, via instinctive behaviour patterns, may well be providing the stimulation the cortex needs to develop, as well as programming a schematic knowledge of these instinctive programmes so the cortex can exercise an influence over their future expression.

Morrison's orientation responses

It was Dement who identified the PGO spikes as the key indicator relating to this drive discharge in the REM state. But, more recently, Morrison (1983) and Morrison & Reiner (1985) showed how these PGO spikes are in fact part of an alerting or orientation response which, in the waking state, accompanies the perception of novel stimuli – turning, for instance, towards a loud noise. This response is associated with an inhibition of behaviour, activation of the cortex and other processes characteristic of the REM state. The intense endogenous production of these orientation responses during sleep may account for many of the phenomena of the REM state itself, and its preparation of the cortex for the processing of anticipated significant stimuli, which in the REM state, at least in the foetus and neonate, may be the release of genetically anticipated stimuli or instinctive behaviour patterns.

Possible implications

Instinctive behaviours can be regarded as inherited schemata (Piaget, 1971) which allow a prepared response to anticipated stimuli which the animal expects to encounter in its future environment. The anticipated stimuli can have their parameters only partially specified in order to allow for the range of variation which individual members of a species may expect to encounter within their habitat. The genetic description of specifically anticipated stimuli has to allow for the range of variation that will be encountered within specific stimuli. The more unspecified the parameters of genetically anticipated stimuli (and responses as well), the greater will be the flexibility in the animal's behaviour, and the greater can be the environmental learning component of the instinctive behaviour.

The diversity of shape, size, composition and location of nests built by birds of the same species shows how wide a variation there can be in the execution of what appears to be a highly controlled instinctive behaviour (Walker, 1983). Consider how many mammals use their unique vocal patterns for mutual recognition of parent and young. The genetic schema cannot include the specific voice pattern that a particular parent or offspring will have. The schema has to be sufficiently indeterminate that any example from the potential range of voice patterns to be encountered by an individual is capable of being selected and recognised as an analogue of that schema. If, then, the sensory parameters of instinctive schemata can, at best, only be partially specified by approximate models, this means that analogues from the world of sensory experience have to be identified to complete the schemata.

As Jouvet noted, there can be little doubt from the

study of monozygotic twins reared together and apart, that the expression of intelligence and personality in humans is to some extent influenced by genetic factors. It is probably fair to say that, for the human species, the parameters of genetically inherited schemata are the least defined. This gives us the widest latitude in the identification of environmental analogues and permits us greater flexibility in the expression of our behaviour.

We know, for example, that there is a genetic substratum to language acquisition, the so-called "language acquisition device" (Vygotsky, 1934), or "deep structure" (Chomsky, 1957). The native language is acquired as a social analogue which completes the genetically programmed language acquisition schemata. Bruner (1986) tells us that it was "Vygotsky's genius to recognise the importance of language acquisition as an analogue".

Suppose a child failed to develop the basic instinctive programmes that underlie human behaviour we would expect that this child would show profound developmental deficits possibly including an absence of language, an inability to relate to people and an inability to learn how to express emotions appropriately. We would also expect to see idiosyncratic and inflexible behaviour patterns. The syndrome that these symptoms typically describe is, of course, childhood autism. Not only do autistic children fail to develop normal human interactions, they do not attend to sounds or visual stimuli in the way normal children do. The autistic child is literally in a world of his own without access to the instinctive templates that would enable him to connect appropriately to his fellow man or his environment. We have previously mentioned Jouvet's theory that instinctive knowledge is programmed during REM sleep. Interestingly a number of studies by Ornitz and his colleagues showed that younger autistic children showed delayed differentiation of the pattern of their EEG compared to normal children of the same age (Ornitz et al. 1976, Cohen 1979).

Asperger syndrome is sometimes regarded as a milder form of autism. The child grows up with normal language and mental development but shows a severe and sustained impairment in social skills. The child clearly lacks the instinctive basis for interpersonal interactions. Without the instinctive templates to guide the development of these skills the child can only be taught external rules to guide them. Unfortunately external rules are a poor substitute for the direct perception of the subtleties involved in social interactions. Consequently these children continue to have major problems with forming and managing relationships.

Because human behaviour and culture shows so much diversity and flexibility, we would therefore expect to find in humans a subtle and sophisticated analogical thinking process to facilitate the identification and assimilation of the cultural analogues. Only such subtlety and sophistication would allow us to complete the genetically influenced parameters of our behaviour patterns and perceptions.

Spearman, in his major work, *The Abilities of Man* (1927), identified two fundamental processes which he called 'education of correlates', or analogical thinking, and 'education of relationships', or abstract thinking. The measurement of analogical thinking ability in some form is now a standard part of almost all intelligence tests (for example, "kitten is to cat as foal is to .....?"). We use analogical thinking to understand and make sense of our world. When we encounter a new experience, we try to find something from our past experience that is analogous to the new one. This applies just as much to scientists trying to make sense of their observations as to ordinary attempts at description or explanation. For example, the analogy of waves is used as one model to make sense of the properties of light. And there was a time not so long ago when the model of the atom was thought to be analogous to planets orbiting the sun.

A special ability of the creative scientist is to make sense of a hitherto puzzling phenomenon by seeing analogies across a wider range of experiences, that is, to make analogies between experiences that most people would regard as disparate. Bruner (1986) gives us a beautiful example of the great physicist Niels Bohr demonstrating just this ability. Apparently Bohr told Bruner that the idea of complementarity in physics arose from the impossibility of considering his son simultaneously in the light of love and in the light of justice! He was in this predicament because his son had just voluntarily confessed that he had stolen a pipe from a local shop. This paradox brought to his mind the trick figure of the vase and the faces often used to illustrate texts on perception. Depending on which aspect you view first, ie figure or ground, you can see a vase or the faces but 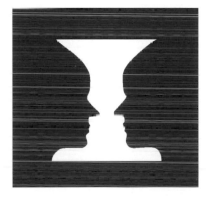 not both simultaneously. He immediately saw the analogy between this situation and the impossibility of thinking simultaneously about the position and the velocity of a particle. This led him on to formulate his complementary principle which says that, if you measure velocity of a particle, this precludes you from measuring its position at the same time and vice-versa.

In this example, we can see that an emotionally arousing introspection enabled Bohr to make sense of this paradox. He sees that the dilemma with his son –

love versus justice – is an analogue of his physics dilemma. This analogue is still a dilemma because he doesn't see a resolution to it. He has now, however, shifted the dilemma into a completely different field, which brings to mind the analogy of the figure/faces paradox. This analogy does suggest a resolution, in that it provides a sensory analogue or model, where we can have mutually exclusive but complementary perceptions of the same object.

The above example illustrates how a great scientist uses analogical thinking to make sense of experience, and in so doing reflects a process that everybody uses to make their experience of the world comprehensible. We try to find analogies between new experiences and our existing schemata. We also use metaphors or analogies to try to convey the subjective quality of our own experience to others. We use analogical thinking as a basic tool in understanding and flexibly communicating the meanings we discern in our experiences.

The charming children's poem below* is an example of how a simple metaphor can identify meaningful related patterns across a wide domain of human experience.

A glove is a house for a hand, a hand.
A stocking's a house for a knee.
A shoe or a boot is a house for a foot
And a house is a house for me!

A box is a house for a teabag.
A teapot's a house for some tea.
If you pour me a cup and I drink it all up,
Then the teahouse will turn into me!

Cartons are houses for crackers.
Castles are houses for kings.
The more I think about houses,
The more things are houses for things.

And if you started in thinking,
I think you will find it is true
That the more that you think about houses for things,
The more things are houses for you.

* We were unable to track down the title or author of this poem. Please get in touch if you know so we can aknowledge in future editions.

52

Barrels are houses for pickles
And bottles are houses for jam.
A pot is a spot for potatoes.
A sandwich is home for some ham.

The cooky jar's home to the cookies.
The breadbox is home to the bread.
My coat is a house for my body.
My hat is a house for my head.

And once you get started in thinking this way,
It seems that whatever you see
Is either a house or it lives in a house,
And a house is a house for me!

A book is a house for a story.
A rose is a house for a smell.
My head is a house for a secret,
A secret I never will tell.

A flower's at home in a garden.
A donkey's at home in a stall.
Each creature that's known has a house of its own
And the earth is a house for us all.

The work of Dement tells us that the development of sensory apparatus in the human foetus and in the new born makes it unlikely that there is a psychical content to their REM sleep. Indeed, the theory which I am developing here would not expect such a psychical content as that must await the identification of the appropriate analogical sensory experience.

What then are we to make of the REM sleep of adults and children which is accompanied by the rich sensory experience we call dreaming?

The model of REM sleep put forward on the basis of the experimental biological evidence suggests that REM sleep in the foetus and neonate programmes instinctive behaviour – genetically anticipated experience. Since the anticipation of sensory experience cannot actually be that specific future experience, it must be an analogue of it. In other words, incomplete schemata are completed by the identification of analogous sensory experience.

Since the dreams of REM sleep have a sensory content, it follows that, if they too are based on anticipated drive schemata, then those schemata must have had a sensory component already assimilated prior to expression in REM sleep. This means that dreams are the analogical expression of anticipated experiences or activated drive schemata from the previous period when we were awake. Dreams must be based on anticipated experiences from waking life that arouse the autonomic nervous system. Because these 'arousals' (active drive schemata) are not deactivated by the anticipated experiences actually happening that day, we carry them into our sleep where they are deactivated by the dreaming process. An activated drive schema from waking, unlike a genetic schema, in order to exist must have a sensory description or content based on the activation of the individual's sensory memory. This means that its release during REM sleep will lead to an analogical sensory experience or dream which, of course, deactivates that drive schemata, as it has achieved its function of sensory representation.

If we consider Morrison's findings of the similarity between PGO spikes and the eye movement potentials of the orientation response, we can see that the release of the activated drive schemata during REM sleep is but a further extension of this similarity. Remember Hunt's idea that the REM state can be seen as a specialised form of the orientation response. He pointed out that the correspondence between the orientation response and the REM state includes not only the similarity of the recordings of the PGO spikes to the recording of eye movement potentials of the orientation response but extends to the cortex, the behavioural inhibition, elevated brain temperature, fixation of attention and hippocampal theta rhythms.

The orientation response prepares the organism to respond to what may be significant new stimuli. Perception is a constructive process and hence we sometimes misperceive people and things – mistakenly thinking we recognise someone, or see objects and shapes that turn out to be different to what we first thought they were. A figure lying in the road on closer inspection can turn out to be a bag of rubbish. In other words, perception is our best informed guess at what we think we are seeing or hearing in a given situation. During sleep, the PGO spikes, as part of an endogenously produced orientation response pattern, alert the organism to process information regarding significant new stimuli. In fact, of course, sensory information from outside is actively inhibited when we sleep (Hobson, 1988). In the absence of outside information, the brain can only base its 'best guess' on significant information that it is actively anticipating – the activated drive schemata – and hence these are released during REM sleep and analogically processed as real perceptions. These are our dreams.

Consideration of the biological research led me to formulate the same hypothesis to explain the origin of dreams derived from my preliminary psychological research reported in chapter 1. This hypothesis has an immense advantage over earlier theories because it is not only applicable to the phylogenetic data – the data from different species – but also integrates the ontogenetic data from foetus to neonate and adult. It makes a specific prediction as to the form of REM dreams – that they are analogical and their origin lies in anticipated experiences or activated drive schemata that remain active at the onset of sleep.

Before reviewing the evidence from a psychological testing of the theory, however, I decided to look at the advantages which this view of REM sleep confers from the viewpoint of evolution. Why did we evolve to dream?

Jouvet (1978) suggested that REM sleep, homoio-thermia and the flexibility of instinctive behaviour are linked. Homoiothermia – being warm-blooded – gave more freedom of behaviour to higher vertebrates and, as they evolved, was accompanied by a "complexification of the brain". Jouvet thought that REM sleep may have evolved to permit more freedom in the expression of instinctive behaviour.

But what exactly were the evolutionary pressures that led to the emergence of REM sleep?

As we know, the ability of mammals and birds to keep a constant internal temperature conferred great advantages on them in terms of mobility. But there was a great price to pay – more than a fivefold increase in basic energy expenditure over cold-blooded creatures. (Karasov and Diamond, 1985). Such a massive increase in metabolism must obviously be compensated for by a corresponding increase in energy supply. This could hardly be achieved by simply extending the time spent looking for food. What was required was a matching increase in productivity, a more productive return between the energy expended in seeking food and the energy gained by acquiring it. One part of this came from cutting down on wasteful time, for example, sleeping when prey or other sources of food were not available. This can be seen as one of the functions of 'slow wave' sleep. But, if one reduces energy expenditure by cutting out non-productive time, although this does conserve energy, it doesn't actually provide it. A massive increase in energy gain is required to compensate for the demands of being warm-blooded. Clearly there was a need to develop the ability to employ this new high-powered energy system in more productive ways.

Such a process or ability needed to be capable, not only of inhibiting particular drives, if the analysis of the organism's total situation vis-a-vis other drives and the external environment should warrant it, but also be capable of motivating continued, directed behaviour by means of goal expectations. This, of course, is the function ascribed to the greatly expanded neocortex in mammals. MacLean summed this up well in 1982 when he wrote: "A remarkable feature of the neocortex is that it evolves primarily in relation to systems receiving and processing information from the external world, namely the exteroceptive, visual, auditory and somatic systems. It was as though the neocortex was designed to serve as a more objective intelligence in coping with the external environment."

For this objective intelligence to operate, it must have a detailed knowledge of, or access to, information about the instinctive programmes. If these instinctive programmes are to allow for individual and environmental variation then this would involve incompletely specified models for which sensory analogues would have to be environmentally identified. The evidence suggests that the function of REM sleep in the foetus and neonate is the programming of these genetically anticipated patterns of stimulation.

This still leaves the further problem that, once a drive schema is activated, it can normally only be deactivated by the actual carrying out of the programmed behaviour by the central nervous system. When the cerebral cortex inhibits an activated drive schema, or when it activates a drive schema through goal expectations and fails to deliver the projected goal, the resources of the cerebral cortex are employed either in inhibiting that programme or in focusing attention towards the achievement of that goal. Clearly, to avoid overloading the information processing resources of the neocortex, which would result in a deterioration of its ability to influence the autonomic nervous system and/or handle newly arising, emotionally arousing, contingencies, it would be advantageous to have a means of deactivating the activated drive schemata which, either because of direct neocortex suppression or because the expectations were not being achieved, remain unsatisfied. REM sleep fulfils this function by allowing the activated drive schemata 'left over' from waking to be vicariously run, thus de-activating them and releasing the data processing potential of the neocortex to deal with the emotionally arousing contingencies of the next period of being awake.

Thus we can see the beautiful economy of nature. The same process that programmes instinctive behaviour – the genetically anticipated patterns of stimulation – are also used to deactivate 'left over' anticipated patterns of stimulation from waking – the activated drive schemata. As the waking anticipated stimulation has a sentient content, its analogical processing in REM sleep leads to a full sensory simulation which deactivates the activated drive schemata. Thus nature accomplishes two essential functions with the same process.

If this theory is correct it leads, of course, to a prediction of the consequences of REM sleep deprivation. It would predict that, if an animal were deprived of REM sleep, this would result in its autonomic nervous system becoming more aroused. This would result in the animal showing a more direct expression of its instinctive drives with increasing inability to control or express instinctive behaviour patterns appropriately. This would also apply, of course, to human beings, although we might expect that social constraints would help people control the expression of those desires. From a phenomenological perspective, we would expect a person deprived of REM sleep to feel that he was being led on by events. His ability to independently analyse and decide for himself matters of personal importance would be impaired and he would be more easily influenced. Also, he would sense an increasing inability to cope with stress (which can be seen as an increase in the numbers or intensities of activated drive schemata). Perhaps this is the reason many of these effects can be observed among members of cults and certain religious orders whose leaders use sleep deprivation to exert control and 'brainwash' believers.

REM deprivation

Many experiments on REM deprivation were carried out on animals and humans in the 1960s and 1970s. Perhaps the most consistent finding was that both humans and animals deprived of REM sleep show a rebound in REM sleep time when allowed to sleep normally following the deprivation. The pressure to have REM sleep was even observed during the deprivation experiments. On the first night seven awakenings at the onset of REM sleep may be sufficient to deprive a subject of REM sleep but by the fifth night thirty awakenings might be necessary to prevent the subject from going into REM sleep. The REM rebound phenomenon therefore seems to indicate a biological pressure, or need, for REM sleep.

Overall though, the results were a disappointment to the experimenters who had expected to see hallucinations and gross personality disturbances. However, the results *were* much in line with what we would expect from the hypothesis developed in this book. For example, REM deprivation resulted in higher autonomic arousal as indicated by the following facts:

• An increase in heart rate from 160 beats a minute to a mean of 200 beats a minute after thirty days of REM deprivation following a lesion in the nucleus pontis caudalis which entirely suppresses REM sleep in the animals concerned (Jouvet, 1965);

• A lowering of seizure threshold for convulsions in rats following REM deprivation for six days (Cohen & Dement, 1965);

• A lowering of the auditory recovery cycle in cats suffering REM deprivation reported by Dewson & co-workers (1967);

• Dement (1967) reported that drive-oriented behaviour was greatly enhanced in cats following REM deprivation (using a mechanical method). The speed of eating was nearly twice as fast as normal and some of the cats showed disturbances of normal sexual behaviour – indulging in compulsive mounting of anaesthetised male cats. Psychometric tests of human subjects showed a significant elevation of expression of need and feeling, together with a significant increase in pathogenic verbalisation (Dement et al, 1976). These findings clearly indicate that REM deprivation results in an increase in autonomic arousal together with an enhancement of particular drive states which is what we would expect if my theory of the origin of dreams is correct.

The effects of REM deprivation on autonomic arousal in humans is much less than in animals. This may partly be because less stressful and efficient methods are used to wake up humans compared with the mechanical methods usually used with animals (Horne, 1988). Hypnotic drugs such as tranquillisers inhibit REM sleep to varying extents, again without any gross disturbances in the behaviour of normal subjects. However, dreaming does occur to some extent outside of the REM state. It may be that REM-suppressing drugs merely displace dreaming into another sleep stage. We also need to know whether these drugs cause a reduction either in number or intensity of the activated drive schemata left unmanifested at sleep onset, thus reducing the need for REM sleep.

Antidepressant drugs also inhibit REM sleep. Interestingly, the therapeutic effects of antidepressant medications may actually depend on their ability to suppress REM sleep. Vogel and collaborators have shown that REM deprivation can in fact be helpful in the treatment of endogenous depression (Vogel, 1979). He also found that those subjects who failed to show an improvement following REM deprivation were also less likely to respond to antidepressant medication. A possible explanation for these findings is that REM deprivation lowers the threshold for triggering drive states when people are awake, thus making it easier for those suffering from endogenous depression to become motivated out of their apathy when awake. Such an explanation would be consistent with the psychobiological approach to the REM state and dreaming developed in this book.

Humans have a much greater neocortex proportionally than most other animals. One role the neocortex plays is to inhibit drive-orientated behaviour and another is to anticipate when that drive-orientated behaviour can be appropriately applied. There is obviously an inter-dependence between the resources of the cortex devoted to inhibiting drive-orientated behaviour and the resources devoted to anticipating the circumstances where that drive-orientated behaviour would be appropriate. This new psychobiological theory of dreams and REM sleep would predict that, to discover the real effect of REM sleep deprivation you would have to study not only human performance on various tasks, but study them in the context of emotionally arousing experiences. When stress levels are increased in number or intensity, this is when we would predict a decline in efficiency of performance as a result of REM deprivation.

Most other theories that seek to account for the function of REM sleep in adults find REM deprivation studies a major problem. But this theory not only explains the effects so far discovered, but also makes specific predictions as to how those effects could be better demonstrated.

We know that the REM state is characteristic of most mammals. It is, however, known to be absent in adult dolphins and perhaps whales. This may well be an adaptation to living in water. The REM state is also absent in the adult of the primitive egg laying mammal, the duck-billed platypus. Interestingly, both these species also have a huge neocortex totally disproportionate to what would be expected. It may well be, as Crick (1983) observed, that this hugely unexpected neocortex may actually be a necessary consequence of *not* having REM sleep. In fact, this theory states that REM sleep is necessary to maximise the efficiency of data processing of emotionally relevant stimuli in the cortex. It would not be surprising, therefore, that the absence of REM sleep would necessitate a corresponding increase in the amount of cortex to compensate.

This theory of REM sleep is applicable not only to humans but to other species as well. It also explains the predominance of REM sleep in the neonate and foetus. It can account for the effects of REM sleep deprivation and predict how those effects could be enhanced. It predicts that analogical thinking would be a major feature of human thinking – which the evidence clearly confirms. The theory also makes specific predictions about the content and form of dreams, and is testable at a psychological level.

Also, for the first time, we have a theory that is not only consistent with the major biological facts of dreaming but also gives us an explanation for the occurrence of symbolism in dreams. Symbolism is one of the most noted phenomena of dreaming yet the major theories put forward so far to explain the recent biological data, such as Hobson and McCarley's activation synthesis theory, or Crick's dreaming to forget theory, cannot explain its occurrence. My theory provides a logically coherent explanation of symbolism in terms of the analogical expression of the activated drive schemata and further predicts that this symbolical (analogical) form will apply to the full content of the dream. The psychological evidence is reviewed next and you will see that it strongly supports the new theory.

Chapter 4

THE PSYCHOLOGY OF DREAMING

Part I: Silberer's autosymbolic effect

THE PSYCHOLOGICAL investigations reported in chapter 2 suggest that dreams arise from emotionally arousing expectations that are not acted out when the dreamer is awake. The emotionally arousing introspections that give rise to these unfulfilled expectations are what I refer to as 'activated drive schemata'.

The hypothesis I've put forward, based on the psychological and biological evidence so far considered, says that these activated drive schemata are translated into sensory analogues during dreaming. It may be possible to accumulate a lot of convincing evidence in support of this hypothesis but, however convincing such evidence might be, we would ideally still like to see a demonstration of this translation process actually taking place. Fortunately such a demonstration is possible.

Foulkes (1962) found that dreaming is not completely confined to the REM state but is recorded from other stages of sleep as well. He suggested that the REM state shows a maximum involvement of the dream production system which can also have a lesser involvement in other sleep states. This idea is also compatible with the evidence that some of the processes of the REM state can be activated at other times.

PGO spikes appear on occasion during other sleep phases outside of the REM state. The analogical thinking that this book suggests is the essence of data processing during REM sleep, would also, of course, manifest itself at other times. Foulkes has noted that short dreams can appear during sleep onset (stage 1 sleep), which is a time when the EEG of the human cortex is similar to that of the REM sleep in humans. Often at this period subjects experience the 'startle response' and jerk awake. The startle response is an intensification of the orientation response manifested with PGO spikes. Foulkes suggested that these less than full blown dream periods, such as occur at stage 1 sleep on occasions, may be a kind of revving up of the dream production engine that could throw light on the dreaming process which is most characteristic of REM sleep.

Surprisingly, the crucial research was already carried out in Freud's lifetime by a colleague of his called Silberer (1909, 1951). Silberer discovered that if he tried to master some anticipated intellectual task when he felt drowsy, a point came when the feeling of drowsiness would temporarily overcome him. He would wake up a few moments later and realise he had dreamt a symbolic representation of his anticipated intellectual task. He called this the 'autosymbolic effect'.

The following five examples make this effect clear.

1   Silberer describes how he is trying to improve a halting passage in an essay. This results in the following dream fragment: "I see myself planing a piece of wood." Here we see the anticipated behaviour replaced with an analogical sensory representation of that behaviour – in the dream fragment he metaphorically smooths out the rough passage in the essay.

2   Silberer is thinking of human understanding as, "probing into the foggy and difficult problem of the 'mothers' in Faust, Part II". This results in the following dream fragment: "I stand alone on a stone jetty extending out far into a dark sea. The water of the ocean and the dark and mysteriously heavy air unite at the horizon." Silberer explains that the jetty extending out into the dark sea corresponds to probing into the problem. The unity of the air and water at the horizon symbolises, as with

the mothers, "all times and places shade into one another, so that there are no boundaries, no here and there, above or below". Again we can see that this dream fragment provides a clear analogical sensory representation of his introspections or anticipation concerning the solution to the proposed problem.

3   Silberer is "trying to think of the purpose of the metaphysical studies I am about to undertake". He decides that the purpose is to "work my way through ever higher forms of consciousness; that is, levels of existence, in my quest after the basis of existence". He then dreams that "I run a knife under a cake as though to take a slice out of it". The cake in question has a number of layers, corresponding to levels of consciousness. The running of the knife through the layers of the cake is an analogy for working through the levels of consciousness. The knife has to be pushed under the cake to remove a slice, corresponding to getting at the basis of consciousness.

Here we have another example of his anticipation being converted into an analogical sensory representation. Silberer called this type of dream symbol a 'material' symbol because it dealt with the material he was contemplating. He also described what he called 'functional' symbolism, which he thought related to the state of consciousness of the dreamer. An example he gives is when he tries to recall what he was thinking about but finds he has lost the connecting link. He dreams of "a piece of typesetting with the last few lines gone". The key point that Silberer's description misses is that the dream sequence is not simply symbolic of his state of consciousness but rather of his introspection or anticipation concerning his state of consciousness. The dream fragment is a sensory analogical representation of his introspection or anticipation of having lost the connecting thread of his argument.

4   Silberer is thinking about something but, whilst "pursuing a subsidiary consideration, departs from the original theme". When he attempts to return to it, he dreams the following fragment: "I am out mountain climbing. The mountains near me conceal the farther ones from which I came and to which I want to return". This dream fragment is a clear sensory analogical represent-ation of his anticipated mental journey.

5   Silberer says: "before falling asleep I want to review an idea in order not to forget". He dreams "suddenly a lackey in livery stands before me as though waiting for my orders". Silberer tells us that, in this instance, he experiences no difficulty in thinking and expects to carry out his task. This example is interesting because it introduces a higher level of complexity than the previous ones. He wants to carry out a certain task and anticipates that he will have no difficulty doing it. His anticipation then includes a reflection of the subject as object, ie there is the self that is anticipating, let's call it self one, that he, self two, will have no difficulty in carrying out the task. In the dream fragment self one is of course himself, the self we are aware of. The livery man waiting for instruction is self two that will be able to carry out the task without difficulty. This dream fragment is again an analogous sensory image of the subject as object willing to carry out the instruction.

Besides material and functional symbolism, Silberer noted a third type of autosymbolic effect arising from somatic phenomena. An example he gives is of a time when he had a sore throat and fever which forced him to swallow saliva steadily. When drifting off to sleep, each time he is about to swallow he sees a picture of a water bottle he is supposed to drink from. Clearly each swallow has become a consciously anticipated behaviour, and the water bottle is a sensory analogy for the mouth holding the saliva.

It is interesting to note in this last example that we are not really dealing with symbols, if we take symbols to stand for something abstract that otherwise can't be represented sentiently. Clearly a mouth with saliva is not an abstract concept. What we are dealing with is a sensory analogical process that can apply both to abstract concepts and sensory concepts.

Silberer was a supporter of Freud and tried to make his findings compatible with Freud's dream theory by arguing that the intellectual apparatus may not be able to support certain ideas for intellectual as well as affective reasons. He suggested that, whenever a thought or idea proved too difficult to be supported by a given state of consciousness, as when we are drowsy, regression to a symbolic thinking process takes place, because this required less effort.

In order to keep his findings compatible with Freud's, he suggested that the symbolisation process could also be caused by Freud's mechanism of repression.

This analysis of Silberer's findings shows that the underlying principle in all his categories is the occurrence of introspections and that these introspections are translated into sensory analogues. This occurs even when the type of thinking involves physical sensations such as swallowing rather than abstract thoughts. What we are observing therefore is a switch over from logical information processing to analogical information processing.

Freud treated Silberer's contribution rather warily in his book, *The Interpretation of Dreams*. He was, of course, aware that it was a two-edged sword. On the one hand, it gives first class evidence for the process of symbolisation taking place. On the other hand, what is being symbolised is straightforward conscious material and not subconscious material that is a threat to the ego, which Freud believed is the function of dream symbolism. It may be for this reason that Freud diverts the reader into a consideration of Silberer's functional symbolism which, as we have seen, is a distinction of little relevance because the same process of introspection underlies all three categories he identified.

The question that needs to be asked is, do we need a second mechanism like Freud's theory to explain dreams or can the process observed in Silberer's research of anticipated experiences being converted into analogous sensory experience during drowsiness (hypnagogic sleep), actually be applied to proper dreams recorded from other areas of sleep? The psychological evidence reviewed in chapter 2, and the analysis of the biological evidence carried out in the last chapter, leads us to anticipate that the same process *is* taking place in dreams proper.

There can be a partial engagement of the dream production system during hypnagogic sleep. This involves a switch from logical to analogical sensory processing of a schema currently being contemplated. During REM sleep, on the other hand, the firing of the PGO spikes in the lower brain stem, triggers the release of the most potent emotionally arousing introspections from waking, and their conversion into analogical sensory based experiences, which deactivate them.

Before leaving Silberer's important work, I would like to point out that his research confirmed two of the main aspects of the theory of dreaming I'm putting forward. Firstly, that the symbolism or analogy relates to the entire dream scene and everything in it. This includes even the dreamer when he has been thinking of 'himself' as the object. (The Freudian view sees only part of a dream, or certain images, as symbolic.) Secondly, Silberer's findings also beautifully illustrate the actual conversion of the emotionally arousing introspections (activated drive schema) into a sensory analogue. Owing to the discovery of Silberer's autosymbolic effect, it is possible to observe both the formation of the activated drive schema and its conversion into a sensory analogue taking place as a continuous whole but which, in REM dreams, are separated in time.

It was my serendipitous rediscovery of Silberer's auto-symbolic effect that prompted my own dream research with the dream described in chapter 2 (dream 1). You may recall that the dream involved me thinking about a traumatic incident from my childhood where I fell off a wall and then dreaming a sensory analogue of that waking recollection where the walls of a castle came tumbling down. I was fortunate that my waking thoughts had involved sensory images as opposed to abstract thoughts. This meant that it was apparent from the start of my research that dream images appeared to involve a translation of certain waking introspections into sensory analogues, rather than simply being pictorial represent-ations of abstract thoughts, as both Hall's and Silberer's work inclined them to suppose.

It was, however, to take me many years before I connected the relationship between images in our minds when we are awake and dream images. During these years I collected hundreds of dreams, both my own and those of relatives, friends and volunteers. By using an alarm clock set at two-hourly intervals, I would wake up a number of times during the night and write down any dreams I could remember. After a time, I became so proficient at this that I would wake up spontaneously four or five times a night and recall dreams. To ensure a representative sample, I would systematically collect my dreams for a period of a week or longer. The dreams were then compared to a detailed examination of my experiences during waking hours. I looked at other people's dreams and waking experiences in the same way to ensure the general applicability of the evidence for this hypothesis.

I found that rarely does a dream on first examination reveal its corresponding waking experience. It is almost impossible for our logical mind to separate itself from the rich sensory immediacy of the dream and consider every element and person (apart from yourself unless considered as object) as a replacement for something else. It is necessary for the logical mind to examine the dream structurally, to ask questions about who such a person could be representing and what a particular behaviour sequence could be representative of from the previous day's experience. If, after such a step-wise examination, the corresponding waking experience didn't suggest itself, and more often than not it didn't, I found it best to leave the problem alone for a while so the analogical thinking process might start to work on it. By consciously thinking about the dream every so often, and what it might mean, then, sooner or later, the analogous waking experience will pop into your head and, on examination, will show that the dream is in fact its sensory analogue. It will be clear that the dream is not simply a sensory analogue of some event from waking but a sensory analogue of our introspections concerning that event.

I can demonstrate this relationship by analysing some fairly straightforward dreams. Then, in the next chapter, I will begin to identify some of the fundamental rules by which this process operates.

Dream 7

I am travelling in a car with my brother. I said that I had made an offer to buy a house in the area and that I had the key in my pocket. My brother was noncommittal about the house as we walked through it. To my surprise there was a huge room at the back of the house. The end wall was completely made of glass and a swimming pool was set in the floor. My opinion of the house's value immediately increased. We went out into the garden and looked at the back. The rear view of the house looked enormous compared to the front. In the dream I never actually saw my brother, I was just aware of his presence.

The previous day I had told my brother about a house I had made an offer on. He expressed reservations about the proposed purchase because he thought the price was rather high. I argued that the area where the house was located was becoming increasingly popular and that a house there could be expected to increase in value in the near future. Although I impressed myself with the argument, my brother remained unimpressed. I reflected to myself that the property might be worth even more than I was offering.

My brother can appear as himself in the dream because I am aware of his presence without actually seeing or hearing him. The dream makes analogically manifest what I anticipated would happen with regard to the house. It does this by letting me show the property, which I made an offer on, transformed to represent the way I had anticipated it would be affected by the changing market. The house increased in size by means of an extra large room, analogous to the anticipated increase in value of the house. The swimming pool is an analogous way of showing that it had gone 'up market'. The rear view of the house was much bigger than the front – with hindsight one could see how much the property and hence the property value had increased. The effect of seeing the extra large room at the rear of the house was to make me increase my valuation of it, just as, in the waking situation, the effect of my anticipation of what the market forces would do to the value of the house made me mentally reflect that the house was probably worth more than I had offered.

We can clearly see, therefore, that this dream in an analogous form simulates experiences which I anticipated when awake but could not experience because the anticipated events lay in the future.

Dream 8

Scene I

> I am walking with someone whom I'm aware must be my wife. We are walking off the main road, through lovely countryside. Suddenly the ground gets marshy. I warn my wife that we must be careful picking our steps and try to get back to the main road without losing our footing.

Scene II

> I go to an experimental theatre, I am aware that I am accompanied by my wife. We arrive early for the play. On the way out we find that members of the staff have pulled back the floors by means of mechanical levers. We have to try to cross the open space by balancing ourselves on the metal bars which supported the floor. I tell one of the young actors to put the floor back and that he should have some manners, as I assumed he had some talent.

The first dream scene represents my initial anticipation of the consequences of buying a house in a particular suburb. Whilst the idea was attractive – like walking through the countryside – it was still a long way from the really popular areas – 'off the main road'. If we didn't 'pick our steps carefully', we might buy in an area where it could later prove difficult to sell and find ourselves on very dodgy ground – 'marshy ground'. This would make it difficult to move back to a popular area if it proved necessary – 'try to get back on the main road'.

The second scene makes manifest other anticipations about looking for a new house that I had when I was awake. I thought we could 'experiment' with looking for a house, although we were starting 'early' – because we couldn't yet afford one. The floor being pulled back analogically represents the floor being taken from under us, which was how I felt when I actually looked at the price of prospective houses. We would have to do a very fine financial balancing act (represented by the physical balancing act in the dream), if we were to proceed further now that the floor was taken from under us (meta-phorically speaking), by the huge cost of houses. On further reflection, I thought to myself, the agents are bound to have a few houses in our price range. There was no need for me to feel embarrassed talking to them. I could afford to be quite assertive. This is expressed analogically in the dream, when I tell the young actor to put the floor back, as I assumed he had some talent, that is, houses in our price range.

You can see that this dream analogically makes manifest those experiences which I anticipated having when my wife and I went looking for houses. In the dream my wife could appear as herself because her presence was intuited rather than directly perceived. This was possible, of course, because she was not playing a direct role in the dream and, consequently, there was no need for her to be perceived.

Dream 9

I'm on a car ferry travelling from Ireland to England. I'm aware that I am a member of a group of undesirable aliens whom the secret service or army would like to arrest and persecute. I huddle into a position in a corner beside my sister. Suddenly, I notice two official looking gentlemen, one in some sort of army uniform jumper and the other in plain clothes, standing near us, although they don't appear to see us. I'm about to leave when a member of my group signals to me to stay where I am. The signal however is ambiguous and I still move off. My sister stays behind as I head in the direction where some of our group are staying at the head of the boat. I am jumped on by the two officials referred to earlier who grab me about the shoulders and say they have already arrested the people I was heading towards.

The dream relates to experiences encountered the previous day when my wife and I went to Windsor Safari Park. I was afraid that the orang-utans would attack and damage the car by leaping onto the bonnet (they would then be more than shoulder high). All the cars were in convoy driving through the compound. We had recently travelled to Ireland and our car, like all the other cars, was driven on to the car ferry in convoy fashion and garaged in compounds. This, of course, was the source of the boat analogy used in the dream. From the point of view of the orang-utans, I felt that we were intruders – 'undesirable aliens'. The car in front of us stopped. It wasn't clear whether we should try and bypass it or stay behind (hence the ambiguous signals in the dream). I suddenly noticed orang-utan on our left. One of them had a thick mane around his neck (which corresponds to the army jumper worn by one of the officials in the dream). (Note also pun with jumper as I was afraid he would jump on the bonnet.) I urged my wife (sister in the dream) to move forward but she seemed unaware of the danger.

In the dream I did actually walk forward, which is analogous to my anticipation when awake of driving forward, but which I could not do because my wife was driving. An orang-utan did actually jump on the car a couple of places ahead of us. When we did begin to move, the two orang-utan near us suddenly became aware of our presence and appeared, to me, about to attack my side of the car. In the dream, the anticipated attack does actually take place – when the two officials grab me about the shoulders. The attack on the car ahead of us corresponds to the sequence in the dream where the officials say to me they have got my friends stationed ahead of me.

Once again we can see a clear analogical relationship between the events of the dream and the emotionally arousing anticipated events of the previous day which did not take place.

Dream 10

> I'm sharing a house with three brothers who are members of the famous pop group, the Bee Gees. One of the three brothers looks much younger than the other two. I like them but I feel a little uneasy, something of an outsider. I'm looking out from the window of the house at two of them playing a game of hurling. I pick up a hurley but I quickly drop it in case they see me as I don't feel myself good enough to play hurling with them.

This dream shows how a television programme can provide the *manifest* content of a dream whilst a second television programme, more closely identified with, can provide the *latent* content of a dream. The manifest content was inspired by a television programme I saw about the Bee Gees returning to England to buy a house and live there. The latent content was inspired by another television programme in which there was a scene with which I strongly empathised. The programme was an episode in a soap opera which glamorously portrayed the world of diamond merchants and dealers. In the series, a family of two brothers and a nephew control the family business. A share in the family business was offered to a key employee. I could not help imagining that, if I were the employee, while I would be flattered by the offer, I would always feel a bit of an outsider and perhaps a little embarrassed to push my own point of view.

The Bee Gees pop group analogically represents the three men involved in the glamorous and lucrative business of diamonds. The house that we are all sharing represents the family business. The game of hurling is an analogy for running a family diamond business. Hurling is a game associated with my youth in Ireland, a national sport which I was never good at and did not enjoy playing competitively. In the dream, the game of hurling I do not participate in expresses the feelings that I anticipated I would have if I were the man in the television programme being offered a share in my employer's family business. It expresses the feeling that I would not be able to participate fully in the 'game' of running the family business, because I was an outsider.

There is also the connection between the fact that only two brothers were playing the game of hurling and the fact that, in the television programme, one brother was a silent partner in the business. The young brother in the dream corresponds to the nephew in the television programme. This dream, therefore, illustrates how the feelings, which are anticipated or introspected upon by empathising with a character in a television programme, are expressed in an analogical form in a dream, thus releasing the resources of the cortex which had been monitoring the environment for the occurrence of suitable stimuli to express those feelings.

Dream 11

There was a Christmas present all beautifully wrapped up on the top of my wardrobe, waiting for

Christmas. There was also a beautiful doll. Daddy got the doll down for me and I nursed it in my arms.

The above dream was told to me by my six-year-old daughter. When I asked her if it was a new doll, she said she'd never held it before but Mummy had let her see it many times. As she recalled the dream she held her arms as if gently holding the doll or a baby and had a beatific smile on her face. She said she could remember exactly how the doll felt to her as she held it in her arms. The previous day her mother had taken her shopping. They had gone to look at prams for the baby which her mother was expecting in seven weeks. The children's toy department was on the same floor. My daughter asked if she could have a toy. Her mother refused because it was not Christmas yet.

The dream is an analogical manifestation of the anticipated events, triggered by this experience: the anticipation of her Christmas present, which is stored on top of our wardrobe until Christmas day arrives (her wardrobe in the dream) and her other anticipation triggered by shopping for the baby. Her mother told her often that she is having this baby for her and encouraged her to feel the baby move when it kicked. In the dream, she analogically represented her mother handing her the baby by getting the doll down from the top of the wardrobe for her. The fact that she knew her mother had let her see the doll many times before, means she was aware of her mother letting her "feel the baby many times before". The fact that her mother is not mentioned means that she was not actually perceived directly in the dream, but she was simply aware that it was her mother who allowed her to see the doll (feel the baby). The baby is due before Christmas and can also be anticipated in its actuality (the doll in the dream) unlike presents which must be wrapped up and remain an unknown quantity until Christmas day.

Dream 12

> I was writing a letter to my husband on striped paper. I realised that it is all wrong to send it on striped paper. It should be more romantic, it should be on flowery paper.

The dreamer of the above dream went on to explain that the pattern of the striped paper corresponded exactly to the lining of her baby buggy. It had been on her mind that her husband had complained a couple of nights previously that, these days, she always wore her unattractive winceyette pyjamas to bed. She wore these pyjamas for the ease of access they gave her for breast-feeding her baby.

Her introspections concerning her husband's complaints led her to realise that by wearing those pyjamas she was sending a wrong message to him that she was more interested in the baby than in romantic experiences. This is analogously expressed in the dream by writing a letter to her husband on striped paper that matches the baby's buggy lining. She realises in the dream that this is all wrong and that she should be writing on "romantic flowery paper".

The dreamer also revealed that the letter she was writing was in the form of a collage rather than writing per se. At the start of the letter she used a picture of an eye to stand for 'I'. This again is an analogous way of showing that her message is a nonverbal one – to the 'eye'. This dream, then, is a clear analogous sensory representation of the dreamer's waking introspections concerning her husband's criticism.

Dream 13

> I'm taking a tube journey. My two oldest sons get
> out at the Park stop. I go on to Mansion House stop.
> I feel awful. I must get back to the Park stop.

The previous day the dreamer had visited a new playschool
to assess whether to register her baby's name for a place
there in the future. The new playgroup was rather
regimented and alien to her artistic temperament (she's
an artist by profession). Later that day a friend praised
the school's discipline methods saying the children were
not allowed to use polish until they had first mastered
how to fold their duster properly. This really made her
even more convinced that the school was unsuitable for
her son and caused her to reflect that she must go and
register her son at the playschool near the park, which
her second son currently attends, and which her eldest
son also attended before transferring to school proper,
also beside the park.

The dream analogically simulates her introspections
concerning these events. In the dream she is taking a
tube journey whereas in real life she actually walked.
Mansion House is the name of a famous brand of polish
and so, analogically, represents the new playschool with
its special attitude towards the use of polish. Mansion
House also sounds very like Manor House which is a tube
station and also the place where her uncle died. Again,
this expresses her attitude towards the new playschool,
which she sees as killing the child's creative impulses.

Her negative feelings towards the new playschool and
her desire to go back to register her son in the park
playschool, which her other sons attended, is analogically
represented in the dream by her unpleasant feelings at
discovering she is on her way to Mansion House, and
that she must get back to Park station where her sons

have already got off. Again, we can see this dream is a clear analogical sensory simulation of her introspection concerning her reaction to her visit to a new playschool.

It can therefore be seen that the 'autosymbolic effect' Silberer identified as operating in the images he saw during periods of drowsiness is identical to the analogical translation mechanism that we have hypothesised is operating in the dreams of REM sleep. Silberer's work provides the great service of demonstrating the actual existence of the analogical sensory translation process, which I was led to hypothesise by my analysis of the biological and psychological evidence.

Chapter 5

THE PSYCHOLOGY OF DREAMING

Part II: Our endless quest for analogy

THE EVIDENCE considered so far comes mainly from three fields: biological, Silberer's work on the dream sequences from the onset of sleep and my own research into dreams. The biological evidence suggests that during REM sleep genetic behaviour may be programmed in the foetus and neonate. We would not expect any such programme to have psychical content, partly because the brain is unlikely to be sufficiently developed to entertain psychical content, and partly because genetic programmes – genetically anticipated patterns of stimulation – of necessity involve only partially specified models to which the animal is programmed to seek a sensory analogue that satisfies, as far as possible, the anticipated parameters of those models.

The more open or less defined the genetic schema, the greater the cultural or environmental learning component. As human beings show the greatest amount of cultural learning and the most flexible behaviour responses, they also ought to show the most sophisticated analogical thinking process. There is substantial evidence, as previously outlined, to support this conclusion.

During REM sleep in the foetus and neonate instinctive behaviours, which are anticipated patterns of stimulation, may be analogically programmed to find suitable sensory analogues for their completion. When dreams start to accompany REM sleep, it seems likely that we are no longer dealing with genetically anticipated schemata awaiting identification of suitable sensory analogues from waking experience. We must be dealing with anticipated schemata from waking life which does, of course, have a psychical content. And, consequently, sensory analogues can be identified from sensory memory when these schemata are released during REM sleep and are being analogically processed as real stimuli. The fact that these released drive schemata are converted into sensory analogues means that they are now completed. They are no longer activated. This frees the resources of the cortex from the task of monitoring the environment in a search for a suitable opportunity to release the drive schemata.

I also noted that REM processes and dream production are not 'all or nothing' phenomena but can show a lesser involvement during stages of sleep other than REM sleep. During sleep onset the brain can go into the analogical data processing mode and a currently conscious schema becomes represented as a sensory analogue. The work of Silberer gave us a number of examples of this process. During REM sleep proper, however, the firing of the PGO spikes, which are the internally generated orientation responses to significant new stimuli, signals the release of emotionally arousing introspections from when we were awake. These are then processed as real stimuli, in the form of sensory analogues, and thus deactivated.

The research I am going to describe next shows further evidence that dreams are introspections made manifest through their analogical sensory simulation.

When we introspect, we model a behaviour sequence or patterns of stimuli which, if accompanied by autonomic arousal, will remain as an emotionally arousing introspection *unless* deactivated by encountering appropriate stimuli, either in real life or as sensory analogues during REM sleep. You will see that there are many reasons why introspections may not be experienced in real life: They may, for example, concern events still in the future; events that were wrongly anticipated; emotionally arousing experiences from the past which have been reactivated as an introspection by some event in the present; or the introspections may concern the experiences of other people in real life, or from television programmes and books that have emotionally aroused us which may then cause us to introspect what those patterns of stimuli would feel like to experience, without, of course, actually experiencing them for real.

Therefore the subject matter of dreams is as complex and varied as our introspective lives and, in fact, allows us to experience our introspection in the form of a sensory analogue – often called symbolism or metaphor.

Let's now look at a number of structurally more complex dreams and analyse them to show how the analogical sensory translation process still operates according to the same rules, however complex the waking introspections may be.

Dream 14

My sister's husband died. My sister was concerned that the paperwork relating to two properties which he had wanted to leave her had not been properly completed. She wanted me to correct the paperwork but I refused saying that it would be wrong and would be immediately spotted.

In the dream I was actually aware of my sister's frustration at the possibility of being disinherited, yet I felt that there was nothing I could do about it. I am quite close to my sister and have always admired her ability to write well. The previous day I had been thinking about two scientific theories I was working on and I reflected that, given the state of my notes, no one would be able to understand the theories if I were to die. I further reflected that, if I were to rush and write up the theories now, I would probably get them wrong. There is, therefore, the 'me'

83

that is imagined to be dead – let's call this self one. There is the 'me' that is imagining that self dead and who is feeling frustration at the thought of the work being incomplete, and who then experiences a desire to complete the work quickly in order to get rid of the feeling of frustration – let's call this 'me' self two. Finally there is the 'me' who, reflecting on this desire of self two, experiences a desire not to carry out this behaviour because it would result in the work being wrongly completed and would be shown to be incorrect by fellow researchers – let's call this 'me' self three.

The dream makes manifest this imagined situation, the three levels of self reflection personified appropriately. There is self one who is imagined to be dead personified by my brother-in-law who has suffered from a heart condition. There is self two personified by my sister who, being the wife of my brother-in-law, is the closest person to him. My sister is also appropriate for this self, as she takes a keen interest in my own research. She and I have a great rapport and it is easy for me to identify with her feelings. This leaves the way clear for the emotions experienced by self three to be actually experienced directly by myself in the dream.

This dream, then, beautifully represents by appropriate analogies the contradictory emotions and levels of self reflection that resulted from my anticipation of my own death.

Dream 15

I am watching a couple, Sam and Janice, committing suicide. Those around them seem powerless to help. They are breathing in carbon dioxide, sitting in their chairs. They seem wrapped up in their own experience. I know I have to, and want to, say something meaningful to them. I think about saying that, if there is a next life, I will see you there, but I am not happy with the phrase. I put my arms around Sam, I say to him, "I love you", then I put my arms around Janice and say, "I love you". Janice reacts and says, "why am I doing this then?" I carry her quickly away from the poisonous gas. I notice Sam has become more alert and I shout to someone to get him too. They are both rescued just in time.

Sam and Janice stand for two clients whom, for reasons of confidentiality, I call Seamus and Sandra. I had been thinking a lot about them the previous day. Their attempted suicide analogically represents the way their emotional problems were killing their happiness (and one of them *had* previously attempted suicide). Two days previously, I had attended an advanced workshop on psychotherapy in which the trainer talked about the importance of not just being a master of techniques but of doing therapy with a "heart". The night before I had been reviewing both Seamus's and Sandra's case notes and was aware of feeling that their next session would be critical for both and hoping I could usefully apply the new therapeutic approach I had learned.

Putting my arms around them in the dream and saying "I love you" is, of course, an analogical way of expressing my anticipation of doing therapy with them – the therapy 'with a heart' that the trainer in the workshop two days previously had talked about. My initial thought of saying "if there is a next life I will see you there" is rejected by me in the dream as this approach appears to be not only 'heartless' but in contrast, ineffective. Therapy with 'a heart' analogically represented by the phrase "I love you" does prove effective in both cases. The words "I love you", actually came from a wedding anniversary card I had bought my wife a couple of days previously. It showed a street of shops and clubs with signs everywhere saying 'I love you'. This phrase appears in the manifest content by virtue of its appropriateness and recent prominence.

Sam stands for Seamus in the dream. Both are of Irish extraction, work with their hands and are of a similar age. Janice represents Sandra in the dream. Both are of English middle class background and have the same qualities of femininity about them. Janice responds first to my intervention in the dream just as in real life Sandra has shown more rapid progress. Sam and Janice both respond to my interventions and their lives are saved, analogous to real life where I anticipated my therapeutic intervention would improve the quality of Seamus's and Sandra's lives.

In the dream I call to someone (whom I don't see) to rescue Sam. I had anticipated in the psychotherapeutic intervention I had planned that Seamus might regress to an incident when young involving someone's death about which he felt guilty. I had planned to have him imagine the dead person giving his views about what happened in a way that would absolve him of his guilt – rescue him. This is the reason why I don't see the person that I call to help him in the dream – because he is dead and the client is going to *imagine* his presence. This dream, therefore, represents an analogical enactment of my anticipated experiences of the previous day concerning two clients' future therapy.

Dream 16

We are going to a party. My family is there. I am walking along the road with my cousin and all our aunts and uncles. We call into a shop for sweets. My cousin gets served but the girl behind the counter doesn't seem to understand my instructions. She keeps getting the wrong bar of chocolate and seems very rude. We go into another shop and I get an old fashioned bag of Maltesers and we eat these small balls of honeycomb covered in milk chocolate. We then see other aunts, and my mother, walking up the road. All my aunts look as though they have been put through a chocolate machine; they all appear as different types of chocolate. I notice that my mother appears as my favourite chocolate. She is some distance behind my aunts. I am annoyed that they are not waiting for her. My family are talking about a skirt that had been given to them by Granny. It is decided to give it to me. I try it on and it fits me perfectly.

The dream is based on the following waking experiences:

1   A member of the dreamer's family had invited her to a party the previous day. The anticipated party provides the setting for the dream.

2   As a senior nurse on her ward round the previous day she had been accompanied by an inexperienced junior nurse who seemed unable to carry out correctly the instructions she gave her and had been rather insolent. This analogy is represented in the dream by her difficulty in getting served by the rude shop assistant.

3   The old fashioned bag of chocolates relates to her weakness for eating chocolate (she had actually bought some on the way home from work the previous evening). The 'old fashioned' relates to her view that this weakness is handed down through the generations in her family.

4   The image of her aunts and mother as bars of chocolate relates to a conversation she had a couple of days earlier with her boyfriend concerning her diet and weight. He said unless she was careful she would continue to put on weight as all her family were overweight – hence her perception of her aunts and mother as bars of chocolate. These ideas were restimulated (ie introspected) by her guilty feelings at buying chocolate on her way home.

5   Another dream theme is the annoyance she feels when she sees her mum falling behind her aunts and her aunts

not waiting for her. This reflects her concern for her mum who had recently had heart trouble. She felt annoyed when she learned that her aunts were rushing to their doctors to have their hearts checked without waiting to see how her mum got on. Thinking about weight led her to recall her annoyance at her aunts' recent behaviour.

6 The final theme is that of the skirt given by her grandmother which fits her perfectly. Her aunts and her mother inherit their figure from her grandmother. The 'perfectly fitting' skirt is an analogy for inheriting the family 'figure' caused through liking sweet things, which she thinks she has inherited.

What is really interesting about this dream is that it seems to be an exception to the rule. All our examples of dreams so far have illustrated the rule that everything perceived in a dream is an analogical representation of something else connected with a waking event. This rule is not, of course, contradicted by those dreams where the dreamer is aware of a person's presence without actually perceiving them in a dream. The difference with this dream is that the dreamer's mother and her aunts actually appear as themselves, but the dreamer's introspection of them as being overweight, as a result of their liking for sweet things, is analogically made manifest by having their bodies turned into different types of chocolate.

This makes clear that what is going on in the dream is not a symbolic replacement in order to disguise identity, à la Freud, but rather an analogical manifestation of the introspected waking perception. Usually this involves the replacing of the waking person by someone else who stands in an analogical similar relationship to the dreamer. But the fact that the body of the person introspected about when awake can be used to express the analogy whilst leaving the person's identity intact, shows that the dream expresses itself in analogies rather than symbolic disguise.

The next two short dreams also show how a person's body can be used to express an analogical relationship with a waking perception whilst letting the person's identity remain the same.

Dream 17

I am pushing a bundle of old branches down to the cellar. The head of the upstairs tenant keeps appearing and disappearing at the centre of the heap of old wood.

The person who told me this dream had been lying in bed the previous evening listening to the noises being made by the upstairs tenant. He tried to dismiss this person from his mind with the thought of what a useless load of rubbish that person was. This is expressed analogically in the dream when he pushes the tenant, in the shape of a bundle of old wood, down to the cellar – the cellar because that is where we store 'old rubbish'. Here again the person's identity stays the same, but their body represents in an analogical form the emotionally arousing introspections concerning how the dreamer views the tenant – as a useless load of rubbish. His attempt to dismiss him from his mind is represented by his pushing him down into the cellar.

Dream 18

I saw a relative lying on a bed. His body was emaciated beyond recognition, only his face was familiar. I told myself that there was no need to worry because he could now start to eat properly again and regain his weight loss.

The previous evening this relative telephoned me and told me that he was going on a starvation diet for forty days. From my knowledge of this person, I knew that any attempt to dissuade him would only make him more confirmed in his action. I reflected that he should survive a month without food and then he could build his strength back up again.

This dream expresses, in the simplest and most obvious way possible, the essence of the introspection. As human thinking is often metaphorical or entails a degree of abstraction, the dream analogue, which has to be expressed as sensory perceptions, appears as a meta-phorical or symbolical representation. The person seen as a load of rubbish, turned into a load of firewood in the dream. Aunts, whose excess weight is seen as caused by eating too many sweet things, are seen turned into different bars of chocolate. In most instances what is anticipated or introspected is not a change in a person's identity or how we imagine them physically: rather the person is part of an anticipated pattern of stimulation and the REM search for an analogue results in replacing all the people and objects in the anticipated or imagined scene with an analogous cast of characters, objects and behaviours.

In every case, the existing model that is programmed in the REM state is treated as though it is an incomplete or approximate model for which a more complete analogue must be sought from the world of sensory memory or experience. The dream just described (dream 18) shows this process at work in the most simple and obvious way. What was anticipated in the waking situation is not a change in the dreamer's or other people's behaviour or personality. There is simply a change in a person's physical appearance. The analogue that is identified during REM sleep does not require a new identity. Instead his present body is changed into an analogous form that would be representative of the anticipated image. In the event, the body image chosen is the sort one sees on television documentaries of starving people in the third world. This dream, then, illustrates clearly the REM process of replacing the 'given' model with an analogically appropriate model using sensory memory.

Dream 19

> Mummy, I was upset last night, I had a bad dream.
> I dreamt I was in the car and it burst into flames.

This dream is included because the analogy with the waking experience is so immediately obvious. The dream was recounted by a twelve-year-old girl with Down's syndrome to her mother, who is a friend of mine. The previous day her daughter had gone on an outing with other children on a hired bus. They had to abandon the bus when smoke started coming from the engine. The dream is clearly an analogical recreation of the experience which the young girl must have pictured in her mind. The bus is replaced by her parents' car. The smoke is replaced by flames – perhaps anticipating that the relief bus which took them home might also be found to have smoke coming from the engine.

The next dream is interesting because it shows how a psychological theory is translated into a sensory analogue.

Dream 20

> I'm walking down the street. I see a man throwing stones. I tell him off. He then directs his attack at me. I run and start screaming for a policeman. The man runs after me. Now there is a policeman on the scene. The man who threw stones starts to talk loudly to the policeman, using emotive language and

blaming me. I reflect I had better speak up quickly or this guy would convince the policeman he was right. I start to shout loudly as well. I'm aware that the policeman can't listen to both of us at the same time, but at least I'm preventing the other guy from winning over the policeman to his viewpoint. The policeman says he will arrest both of us if we don't sort it out between us. I talk to the other guy and explain what the policeman said because he obviously didn't understand what was said. He is then prepared to be friendly.

I go into the car park to get my bicycle as I live some distance outside the town. I find that my bicycle isn't there and I must have left it at home. I can't remember how I got into town. I must have got a lift from someone else, without thinking how I was going to get home. I realise that, without my bicycle, I have no means of getting home. I walk out of the car park and as I do so, I repeat to myself the sentence that I used to explain to the other fellow what the policeman had meant. The fellow is walking behind me and he repeats what I said. I feel embarrassed and ignore him.

The previous evening I had been reading a book on the lateralisation of the brain by Blakeslee (1980) which describes studies showing that the left and right cerebral hemispheres process information differently.

I read of a patient who had undergone the split brain operation (severing of the corpus callosum which joins the left and right cerebral hemispheres together, in order to relieve severe epilepsy) whose right hand signalled his wife to come and help, even as his left hand pushed her aggressively away. It seems that strong emotions may be more associated with the right hemisphere. The right hemisphere, of course, controls the left side of the body and vice-versa.

I read of another patient who had his right cerebral

cortex completely removed and who, as a consequence, was unable to find his way back from the bathroom. Other examples were given which showed that spatial intelligence and sense of direction is primarily a right hemisphere activity. Right hemisphere activities also appear to be more involved in motor skills such as getting dressed. Following certain tests designed to stimulate the right hemisphere, subjects were observed to go into a dreamy state where they spoke little, sometimes not even responding to their own name, but carried out the tests even more efficiently. It seemed as though the subjects had gone into a trance state. Left hemisphere consciousness (our normal state) on the other hand is much more sensitive to speaking and comprehending language with a skill not possessed by the right hemisphere. (To talk of 'right and left hemisphere consciousness' is to take speculation beyond that justified by the experimental evidence in the view of many psychologists. My dream is not concerned with an objective view of the evidence but rather with my subjective reactions to the views presented in Blakeslee's book.)

The two hemispheres compete for dominance at any one time. As the left hemisphere has a slight genetic advantage for language development (except in a small percentage of left handers), it becomes primarily the language brain whilst the right hemisphere becomes more able at processing spatial data. Usually the hemisphere that is best qualified for a particular task takes control.

Finally I read about stuttering. Experimental evidence was cited which showed that some stutterers don't have a well defined left hemisphere dominance for language. In the book, Blakeslee quotes a study by Jones (1966) of four patients who had stuttered since childhood. Each of the four had a damaged speech area on one side of the brain. The damage was of recent origin and unrelated to stuttering. A Wada test showed that the speech was controlled by *both* hemispheres; after the damaged area was surgically removed, the patients ceased stuttering and regained normal speech. The patients' stuttering was evidently caused by both hemispheres having developed a capacity to control speech. A post-operative Wada test showed that speech was now controlled by one hemisphere only. It was easy to imagine that the false starts which a stutterer makes when he tried to speak could be caused by both speech areas trying to speak at once.

The dream makes manifest my introspection concerning these aspects of brain lateralisation, as the following points make clear:

1   The man throwing stones as I walk down the street represents the aggressive potential of the right hemisphere as in the example of the 'split-brain' man whose left hand tries to attack his wife, even as his right hand seeks her help. I reprimand the man in the dream representing the left hemisphere, which is what I imagined the previous evening would actually happen in that situation.

2   In the next dream scene, I call a policeman representing 'control of the brain'. When the policeman arrives the stone-throwing man talks loudly in emotive language to try to get the policeman to accept his version of events. The man's emotive language represents the right hemisphere's better ability to understand the emotive connotations of language. I (the left hemisphere consciousness) realise that I will have to compete with this guy if I am to prevent the policeman from accepting his viewpoint. This scene analogically represents the competition between the two hemispheres to win control. The policeman says that, if we can't sort it out between ourselves, he will arrest both of us (arrested development).

3   I (left hemisphere) have to explain to the man (right hemisphere) the meaning of what the policeman has said, thus analogically demonstrating the left hemisphere's better language comprehension and expression. Following my explanation, the right hemisphere is prepared to be friends, analogically demonstrating that the hemisphere best qualified to take charge, usually does.

4   In the next scene, I go into the car park to get my bicycle only to find that it's not there and I have no idea how I arrived there or how I'm going to get back. I assume someone else (right hemisphere) must have given me a lift. This scene analogically represents the left hemisphere's dependence on the right hemisphere's superior spacial ability and sense of direction. In explaining the unconscious mind I often use the example of riding a bicycle as an acquired skill that has become an unconscious motor programme, something we do without thinking about it. In the same way, Blakeslee suggests we depend on the right hemisphere to take us to and from familiar places without having to think about it. In the example given in the book the person who had their right hemisphere removed could not find their way back from the bathroom. At first it seems rather surprising to look for a bicycle in a motor car park, until we realise that the dream is using the motor car park as an analogical image to represent the right hemisphere's greater involvement in our unconscious motor programmes which the brain has acquired, such as cycling and getting dressed. Note also that we look for a 'space' to park our motors in a car park, and these programmes are concerned with spatial intelligence.

5   The final scene represents the last point in my previous night's reading that I introspected about, namely the possible influence of brain lateralisation on the development of stuttering. When a person stutters they

repeat the same syllable or word over and over again. This is represented analogically in the dream when I repeat the same sentence I had said previously. This sentence is repeated again by the stone-throwing man following me – my 'right hemisphere'. This scene then is an analogical representation of the stutterers having language ability controlled by both sides of the brain and the dual control causing interference by repeating the same words or syllables. The fact that I (left hemisphere) say the sentence twice, and the right hemisphere, represented by the man following me, repeats the sentence only once, analogically demonstrates the greater involvement of the left hemisphere in language production. In the dream I feel embarrassed by the repetition of the sentence and ignore it. This is what the stutterer usually does, he presses on with what he is trying to say despite his embarrassment caused by the repetition.

When I first recalled this dream in the early morning, I thought it was an incomprehensible jumble of images, but from previous experience I know that this is a typical and misleading reaction derived from our left hemisphere's logical thinking. The ability to discover analogies seems to be a right hemisphere activity. I forced myself to record the dream before I forgot it. When I started to think about the possible meaning of the dream a little while later, and also reflected on what I had done the previous day, I quickly saw the analogy with my reading about the left and right hemispheres. I didn't see all the analogies straight away. But I stimulated my analogical thinking process by thinking about the dream's possible meaning, and then waited to see what would result. A couple of hours later the meaning of the car park – a parking place for motor programmes – flashed into my mind. A little later the meaning of the repeated sentence – its analogical relationship to stuttering – flashed into my mind.

The decoding of the dream's analogies requires the ability to break down the dream into individual scenes and to consider what the possible meaning of those scenes could be in the light of our previous day's activities. This process will stimulate an on-going analogical search that may lead to the discovery of where the meaning lies. Finally, we have to compare the individual components of the dream to the components of the introspective waking experience we identify to see how good the fit is. Sometimes the fit is simply not good enough and components are left unmatched. Then the analogical search has to continue until a satisfactory match between the components of the two patterns are found. Only then can we be sure that we have identified the analogous waking introspective experience on which the dream is based. When we consider dreams and creativity you will see that these processes are similar to the processes involved in creative discoveries and problem solving.

Since this particular dream is concerned with the relationship between the right cerebral cortex and the left cerebral cortex, this is an appropriate place to consider a study by Hoppe, published in 1977, relevant to this point. He reports on a study of twelve commissurotimised patients (patients whose corpus callosum is severed) together with another patient (Mrs G) whose right cerebral hemisphere had to be totally removed because of recurrent glioma. Mrs G reported a dream in which a doctor and a psychiatrist drove her to a restaurant and treated her to a lobster and martinis exactly as it had happened in waking life. My theory would lead me to suggest that Mrs G must have relived the experience in her waking imagination and, consequently, the experience became manifest in a dream but, without a right cerebral hemisphere, it was not translated into an analogical experience. This finding fits neatly with the evidence that the right cerebral cortex is biased in favour of processing analogical and metaphorical thinking, whilst the left cortex is biased in favour of digital language and logical analysis (Bogen, 1969, Watzlawick, 1978).

Hoppe's study of the twelve commissurotimised patients' dreams showed that their dreams appeared to be conscious daydreams without symbolisation. If this observation is correct it again suggests waking introspections giving rise to dreams which, as a result of severing the right hemisphere from the left, may retain their original format and are not, therefore, converted into analogical sensory experiences.

Normal dreaming, therefore, demonstrates our right hemisphere's endless quest for analogy continuing even in sleep.

Dream 21

I am trekking through America with David Niven and a younger man. Presently I am in a toilet with a door which is half made from glass. School children can look in. I see some blood on my clothes and I realise my period has started. I go into a shop to purchase sanitary towels. The shop assistant was not very helpful. He tries to sell me things I don't need and seems reluctant to sell me what I want. By the time I get what I want, I am getting very worried as it is getting very late and dark outside.

The subject who told me this dream thought it was related to a television play she saw the night before, in which a school teacher appeared to rush out of the classroom because her period had started. The television programme provided part of the analogy expressed in the manifest content of the dream but more importantly it served to reactivate for her the memory of the traumatic events of previous weeks. The dream deals with events which she anticipated might have happened and the emotions stimulated by the anticipation of those events during the preceding few weeks. The dream can be analysed as follows:

David Niven represents her husband in the dream. He was at that time reading a biography of David Niven. Although, unlike her husband, David Niven was an old man at this time, this can be seen as a pun for her 'old man'. The younger man stands in for her young family doctor with whom they had started a series of investigations to find out the cause of their infertility – hence the trek through America, land of pioneers and explorers of unknown territory.

A few weeks previously at the hospital where she worked as a staff nurse, she suddenly developed a severe pain in her pelvis and had to stop work. (Note the analogy with the television programme where the young teacher rushes out of the classroom because her period had started.) She was admitted to a ward with a door which had shutters on the outside which could be pulled back allowing the nurses to look in. These nurses were mainly student nurses. The door with the shutters, which the student nurses could pull back and look through, is analogically expressed in the dream by the half glass door which the school children could look through.

The unhelpful shop assistant refers to the medical registrar who continued to explore a diagnosis of ectopic pregnancy, despite her conviction that this could not be the case. The subsequent operation showed that she had endometriosis involving the rupturing of blood-filled cysts near her reproductive organs, hence the analogy of her period starting. In the dream she starts to get worried when she realises it is getting late and she is still waiting for the correct article to absorb the blood. In the real life situation she was discharged from hospital and an operation was scheduled for the following week. Continued pain, whilst waiting for the operation, made her fear that the operation might come too late, hence her worry in the dream that it is getting late and dark outside.

We can see, therefore, that the dream expresses in analogical form her reactivated anticipation or introspection of the events leading up to her operation. The memory of those traumatic events in the recent past was reactivated by an event in the present – the television play.

In the next chapter we will see that Freud's 'specimen dream' of 'Irma's injection' follows exactly the same pattern and, had Freud realised this fact, he would instantly have been able to disprove his own theory of dreams.

Chapter 6

TWO CARD HOUSES

The seminal dreams of Freud and Jung

FREUD'S SPECIMEN dream, known as "the dream of Irma's injection", is the key dream sequence in Freud's book *The Interpretation of Dreams*. Fortunately the relevant historical evidence about the traumatic events in Freud's life over the months preceding this dream, and the trauma reactivated on the night before by the remarks of a visiting friend, are available to us. This evidence provides the key to understanding his dream in the light of what I have suggested about the purpose of dreams. We shall see an explanation that is far removed from the explanation arrived at by Freud himself. It was, in fact, a precise metaphorical re-enactment of specific historical events in his life concerning which he was much troubled. The dream was described by Freud as follows:

> A large hall – numerous guests, whom we were receiving – among them was Irma. I at once took her on one side, as though to answer her letter and to reproach her for not having accepted my solution yet. I said to her: If you still get pains it's really your own fault! She replied: if only you knew what pains I've got in my throat and stomach – it's choking me – I was alarmed and looked at her. She looked pale and puffy. I thought to myself that after all I must be missing some organic troubles. I took her to the window and looked down her throat, and she showed signs of recalcitrance like women with artificial dentures. I thought to myself that there was really no need for her to do that – she then opened her mouth properly and on the right I found a big white patch: at another place I saw extensive whitish grey scabs upon remarkable curly structures which were

evidently modelled on the turbinal bones of the nose – I at once called Dr M and he repeated the examination and confirmed it. Dr M looked quite different from usual, he was very pale, he walked with a limp and his chin was clean shaven... My friend Otto was now standing beside her as well, and my friend Leopold was percussing her through her bodice saying : She has a dull area low down on the left. He also indicated that a portion of the skin on the left shoulder was infiltrated (I noticed this as he did), in spite of her dress... M said "there's no doubt about it it's an infection, but no matter, dysentery will supervene and the toxin will be eliminated" ... We were directly aware, too, of the origin of the infection. Not long before, when she was feeling unwell, my friend Otto had given her an injection of a preparation of propyl propyls, ... propionic acid... trimethylamin (and I saw before me the formula for this printed in heavy type)... Injections of that sort ought not to be made so thoughtlessly... and probably the syringe had not been clean.

Freud had this dream on the night of the 23rd-24th July 1895. He regarded it, and his interpretation, as so significant that he called it his 'specimen dream' and devoted some fourteen pages in *The Interpretation of Dreams* to its analysis. He even wrote to his close friend Fliess on the 12th June 1900: "do you suppose that some day a marble tablet will be placed on the house, inscribed with these words: In this house on July 24th 1895, the secret of dreams was revealed to Dr Sigmund Freud".

From Freud's discussion of the background to the dream we know that on the previous day he received a visit from an old friend who was also the family paediatrician, Dr Oskar Rie. Earlier in his career he had been Freud's assistant and collaborated with him on a scientific paper. In Irma's dream Freud calls him Otto.

Otto had come directly from Irma's home where he had been staying with her and her family. Freud asked him how Irma was and he replied, "she's better but not quite well". Freud was annoyed by Otto's reply as he fancied that he detected a reproof in the reply to the effect that he (Freud) had promised the patient too much. He gave no indication to Otto of his feelings but that night he worked late, writing out a case history to give to Dr M (Dr Josef Breuer, a senior colleague and a collaborator with Freud on a book on hysteria).

Freud goes on to give lengthy associations to each element in the dream and, finally, concludes that the main instigating force for the dream was a wish to exonerate himself from any blame for the lack of complete success in the treatment of Irma's condition. This is achieved by (a) blaming Irma herself for not accepting his solution, (b) pointing out that, because the pains were organic in nature, they were not treatable by psychological means, and (c) implying that Otto had caused the pains by giving her an injection with a dirty needle. These reasons are not, however, as Freud himself noted, mutually applicable. The dream also gave him his revenge on Otto by making Otto responsible for Irma's condition.

Now that we are aware that all the elements in a dream stand for something else, with the exception of where someone's presence is felt but not perceived, we can conclude that Freud's explanation for the dream, based as it is on the manifest characters, is wrong. Furthermore, on the basis of a paper by Schur (1966) in which previously unpublished letters of Freud to his friend Wilhelm Fliess are included, we can with some certainty identify the true meaning of Freud's specimen dream.

We learn from these letters that Freud had treated a young woman named Emma Eckstein, a spinster aged twenty-seven, in March 1895 for hysterical nose bleeds.

He called his friend Fliess, a nose and throat specialist, to examine her to see if there was a somatic basis to her illness. Fliess had not only operated on Freud himself but was also at this time Freud's major confidant and expressed complete confidence in Freud's theories. Fliess travelled from Berlin to Vienna to examine Emma and operated on her nose on the 4th March. Freud wrote to Fliess telling him that the swelling and bleeding hadn't let up and that a foetid odour had set in. He goes on to say that he called in another surgeon, G, who inserted a tube to help the drainage.

Four days later he writes again to Fliess telling him that profuse bleeding had started again and, as surgeon G was unavailable, he had called in surgeon R to examine Emma. While cleaning the area surrounding the opening, R began to pull at a thread and suddenly at least half a metre of gauze came away from the cavity. This was followed by profuse bleeding. Fliess had left a piece of iodoform gauze in the cavity some two weeks earlier which had interfered with the healing process and was the source of the foetid smell. He goes on to say that the leaving in of the gauze was an unfortunate accident that could have happened to the most careful surgeon and he reassures Fliess of his complete confidence in him.

On the 28th March 1895 he again wrote to Fliess reassuring him about Emma's condition but, by the 11th April, he is again writing to Fliess telling him that Emma's condition has deteriorated, there was a further highly dangerous haemorrhage and that these were "gloomy times, unbelievably gloomy" and that he was "really very shaken".

On the 20th April Freud replies to a letter from Fliess, telling him that his (Fliess's) suggestion that they could have waited was completely impractical. Indeed, if the surgeon had sat around and waited, Emma would have "bled to death in half a minute". However, he goes on to reassure Fliess that he remains for him "the prototype of the man in whose hands one confidently entrusts one's life and that of one's family".

These traumatic events occurred some four months prior to the Irma dream of the night of the 23rd July 1895. As we can see from his letters these were profoundly anxious times for Freud. A patient was in danger of losing her life as a result of a mistake made by a surgeon he had recommended who also happened to be (at that time) his closest friend. Freud's confidence was badly shaken.

Indeed we may well suspect that it was because of these traumatic events that he was so sensitive to what he felt was an implied rebuke in his old friend Otto's remark about Irma's treatment. No doubt his reaction of staying up late to write out her case history in order to justify himself, also helped to bring back in full force to his mind these traumatic events. In fact, as Schur noted when he published these letters of Freud to Fliess, there were many resemblances between the traumatic events recounted in the letters and Freud's dream of 'Irma's injection'. Without the benefit of the theory I have now put forward, he was, perhaps, unlikely to do the full structural comparison necessary to show that the dream of 'Irma's injection' is a precise analogical restatement of the traumatic events of Emma's treatment. It is a re-enacted analogical scenario of those events with Freud's introspected views about Fliess's blame made abundantly clear to everyone, including Fliess.

The setting for the dream is the party to be held the next day to celebrate his wife's birthday. Among the guests is Irma, who Freud takes aside to rebuke for not having accepted his solution. Freud tells us that Irma (a name used by Freud to protect the patient's identity) was a young widow and a friend of the family. Masson (1984) produced evidence from a number of sources which identify Irma as Anna Hammerschlag, a young widow whose husband died a year after their marriage, and who was the godmother of Freud's daughter Anna. She was briefly treated by Freud at this time. This manifest dream character of Irma-Anna was an analogical replacement for Emma Eckstein as will become clear.

Freud's friend Fliess propounded a bizarre theory that the nose and sexual organs were intimately connected and that somatic symptoms, allegedly arising from masturbation, could be cured through nasal surgery. Both Irma-Anna and Emma were referred by Freud to Fliess for nasal examination. Fliess as we have seen recommended and carried out nasal surgery on Emma Eckstein, to remove the turbinate bone in her nose with near fatal consequences. Fliess, who was at that time an inexperienced surgeon, advocated this entirely unnecessary operation on the grounds that it would help her recover from what his theory said were the harmful effects of masturbation. Following the operation Fliess returned to Berlin. No doubt Freud was irritated, as in the dream, when following the operation she still complained of somatic symptoms. When he examines Irma in the dream she shows signs of recalcitrance; in his letter to Fliess of the 4th March 1895, he tells him that he encountered "resistance to irrigation".

The throat in the dream is, of course, an analogy for the nose. This is made quite clear in the dream when he looks down her throat and sees structures similar to the turbinal bones of the nose. Freud tells us that it was Fliess who had drawn scientific attention to the relationship between the turbinal bones and the female sex organs. Freud goes on to tell us in the dream that his examination revealed "a big white patch" and "whitish grey scabs" upon these structures, ie the operation site. He at once calls in

Dr M (from his association to the dream this is known to be Dr Breuer), a senior colleague of his, who confirms his examination. This parallels the events recounted to Fliess in his letter of the 4th March 1895, where he says that because of the pain and oedema he let himself be persuaded to call in Dr Gersuny who said that access to the cavity was restricted and inserted a rubber tube to help drainage.

Freud notes that Dr M did not have his usual appearance but possessed the physical characteristics of his older half brother. In his letter of the 8th March, Freud tells Fliess that Dr Gersuny had behaved in a rather rejecting way towards him during his visit. This explains why the character in the dream standing for Gersuny, is a composite of Dr M and Freud's half brother, both of whom, Freud tells us in his associations to the dream, had recently rejected a suggestion which he had put to them.

We are next told that Otto was standing beside the patient. Otto (Dr Oskar Rie) is the analogical replacement for Fliess in the dream. It's not surprising that Otto should have been Fliess's analogical substitute. Both men were friends of Freud, both were doctors, both had a professional relationship with Freud and his family and both had been involved in Freud's theoretical work.

Following the visit of Dr Gersuny – Dr M of the dream – Freud wrote a series of letters to Fliess making him aware of each step in the developing crisis. We can see therefore, how, in a metaphorical sense, he was standing beside the patient. In line with this view, Otto doesn't do anything from this point except observe what is going on.

Next in the dream sequence, we learn that Freud's friend Leopold is examining Irma. In Freud's letter of the 8th March 1895 we learn that he had to call in a Dr R to examine the patient because Dr G wasn't available. We can see that the structure of the dream is working out exactly as it did in real life. In the dream, Dr Leopold's examination indicates that a portion of the skin on the left shoulder was "infiltrated". Freud could see the infiltration in spite of Irma's dress. In the real life situation, Dr R pulled at something like a thread and a piece of gauze was removed – an "infiltration" as it was a "foreign body" (Freud's phrase as used in his letter) that should not have been left there from Fliess's operation.

Following this incident in the dream, Dr M intervenes again and gives the opinion that, "there's no doubt it's an infection..." etc. We have already shown that Dr M (Breuer) is the analogical substitute for Dr Gersuny and, in real life, we again know from Freud's own letter of the 8th March to Fliess, that Dr Gersuny did come the next day and assist Dr R in attending the patient.

We come next to perhaps the most important element of the dream sequence. Freud says: "We were directly aware too of the origin of the infection. Not long before, when she was feeling unwell, my friend Otto had given her an injection of a preparation of propel, propyls... propionic acid ... trimethylamin (and I saw before me the formula for this printed in heavy type)... injections of this sort ought not to be made so thoughtlessly... and probably the syringe had not been clean".

The first thing to note is the time sequence "not long before". In other words, *before* the sequence of visits analogically represented in the dream which, of course, corresponds exactly to the sequence in real life. Fliess had carried out his abortive operation *before* the sequence of other doctors' visits were set in train. Everybody in the dream, including Otto (ie Fliess), is aware that Otto is to blame, that he had been thoughtless and probably negligent in that the syringe wasn't clean. Freud may have felt protective towards his close friend Fliess, following the discovery of Fliess's mistake, as indicated in his letters to him. The dream, however, makes clear that, by the night before the dream, Freud had come to see that Fliess had been professionally negligent, and that the other doctors who were subsequently called in, were also aware of Fliess's professional incompetence. It would have been natural for Freud to review these events, from the point of view of who was to blame, on the night before his dream, as he was concerned that night with writing a defence of his own professional conduct in the case of another patient, whom he had also referred to Fliess for treatment.

The injection of "propionic acid... trimethylamin" is again an analogy. Propionic acid is described in pharmacological reference books as having a 'putrid and rancid odour'. Freud in his letter to Fliess describes Emma's lesion as having a 'foetid' odour. Medical friends have told me that gauze left overly long in a wound gives rise to a 'particularly foul smell of rotting flesh'. The trimethylamin again refers to Fliess. He had told Freud that it was one of the products of sexual metabolism. Fliess's operation removed the turbinate bone in Emma's nose in order to alleviate the deleterious effects of masturbation which he claimed gave rise to a 'nasal reflex neurosis'. We can see that this formula points the finger of blame at Fliess for being responsible for the foul smelling lesion in Emma's nose which resulted from his abortive operation.

Freud's dream of 'Irma's injection' is, therefore, a metaphorical simulation of the traumatic events of the 'Emma affair' in which everybody is made aware of where the blame really lies – with Fliess. It is also apparent that Freud's sensitivity to the assumed criticism of his professional conduct, implied by Otto's remarks of the night before, reawakened the trauma of his recent involvement in the 'Emma affair'. This patient nearly lost her life following her referral, by him, to his friend Fliess for unnecessary and unorthodox surgery. Just as he wrote the case history of Irma that night to make clear that he was not responsible for her continuing symptoms (recall that he had also referred her to Fliess), so the dream also makes clear that it is Fliess and not himself who is responsible for the mistreatment of Emma. In fairness to Freud it should be noted that he had complete faith, at that time, in what he thought was Fliess's unrecognised genius and that his referral of patients to Fliess was done in good faith.

Little wonder then that Freud was so sensitive to what he saw as the implied criticism, made by his friend Dr Oskar Rie, of his treatment of their mutual friend Irma. Indeed, Freud felt *so* sensitive to this 'criticism' that he stayed up to write her case history. The case of Emma Eckstein cannot have been far from his mind as he addressed that case history to his mentor Dr Breuer in order to, in his own words, 'defend myself'. He had referred both patients to his friend Fliess and one of them nearly lost her life as a result of Fliess's bizarre theories and incompetent surgery. Freud's introspections about that nearly fatal case, including his acknowledgement of Fliess's blame, are analogically expressed in his dream of 'Irma's Injection' exactly as predicted by the theory of dreaming presented to you now in this book.

By good fortune we have enough information to establish the real meaning of another famous dream, this time dreamt by Jung. This dream, and his interpretation of it, was as important in the development of Jung's theories, as Freud's interpretation of the dream of 'Irma's Injection' was in his.

In his biography (1964) Jung says: "One (dream) in particular was important to me, for it led me for the first time to the concept of the collective unconscious". The dream is as follows:

Jung's house dream

I was in a house I did not know, which had two
storeys. It was "my house". I found myself in the
upper storey, where there was a kind of salon
furnished with fine old pieces in Rococo style. On
the walls hung a number of precious old paintings.
I wondered that this should be my house and
thought "not bad". But then it occurred to me that I
did not know what the lower floor looked like.
Descending the stairs, I reached the ground floor.
There everything was much older. I realised that this
part of the house must date from about the fifteenth
or sixteenth century. The furnishings were
mediaeval, the floors were of red brick. Everywhere
it was rather dark. I went from one room to another
thinking "now I really must explore the whole house."
I came upon a heavy door and opened it. Beyond it,
I discovered a stone stairway that led down into a
cellar. Descending again, I found myself in a
beautifully vaulted room which looked exceedingly
ancient. Examining the walls, I discovered layers of
brick among the ordinary stone blocks, and chips
of brick in the mortar. As soon as I saw this, I knew
that the walls dated from Roman times. My interest
by now was intense. I looked more closely at the
floor. It was of stone slabs and in one of these I
discovered a ring. When I pulled it, the stone slab
lifted and again I saw a stairway of narrow stone
steps leading down to the depths. These, too, I
descended and entered a low cave cut into rock.
Thick dust lay on the floor and in the dust were
scattered bones and broken pottery, like remains of
a primitive culture. I discovered two human skulls,
obviously very old, and half disintegrated. Then I
awoke.

Interestingly, Jung was on a voyage to America with Freud
in 1909 when he had this dream. On hearing the dream,
Freud pressed Jung to uncover any wishes in connection

with the two skulls, obviously thinking that a death wish was the key to understanding it. Jung reports that, to satisfy Freud, he lied and said that they reminded him of his wife and sister-in-law. Freud appeared relieved on hearing this; no doubt because he thought Jung wasn't harbouring a death wish against him.

To Jung the house represented an image of his psyche. At the beginning of the dream he is on the first floor, the salon, which represents normal consciousness. The remaining floors represent different levels of consciousness. The cave represents the most primitive level of all, the consciousness of primitive man, which still lies buried in our unconscious. It was but a short step for Jung to go from this analysis to his idea of a 'collective unconscious' – a common store of vague racial memories and archetypes. Jung thought that these archetypical images could surface in dreams.

We are fortunate, as in the case of Freud's dream, in having details of what preoccupied Jung in the days prior to the dream. In his biography, Jung tells us that, "certain questions had been on my mind". Those questions were: "on what premise is psychology founded? To what category of human thought does it belong? What is the relationship of its almost exclusive personalism to general historical assumptions?"

For Jung to be so preoccupied with these questions means that he introspected a lot about them, an activity that would result, according to my theory, in dreams about his imagined explorations of these questions. It will become clear that Jung's dream is just a metaphorical exploration of the last question, namely psychology's relationship to historical assumptions. Jung's exploration of the house in the dream is a metaphor for his introspective exploring of this question.

The house, as Jung saw clearly, is a metaphor for the

psyche. The dream starts off with Jung being in a house he doesn't know, but yet it is his own house. The fact that the house is his own house represents the 'almost exclusive personalism' aspect of the question which Jung is exploring. That is, the house is his personal property just as the psyche is also a personal attribute. Yet he doesn't know the house, just as in real life he doesn't yet know the answer to his question about the psyche.

Each floor of the house corresponds to a different historical period. At the start of the dream Jung finds himself on the first floor, corresponding to the most recent historical period. This is quite a civilised period, as can be seen from the eighteenth century-style "fine old pieces" of furniture together with "precious old paintings" suggesting that the contribution from the great masterpieces of the past were retained and valued in this period. The fact that the furnishings, as Jung noted, are mainly eighteenth century and rather old fashioned suggests that Jung saw a time lag between historical influences and their manifestation in the psyche. As Jung descends through the floors, the age of the building goes back further and further into the past. On the ground floor he finds that this part of the house must date from the fifteenth and sixteenth century. The furnishings are mediaeval and the floors are made of red brick. The fact that everywhere was rather "dark" reminds us that we are dealing with "the dark ages", stretching from the mediaeval period back to the end of the Roman empire.

Jung next goes down a stone stairway that leads to the cellar. He notes that the walls date from Roman times, made as they were from 'stone blocks' and mortar which had 'chips of bricks' in it. The fact that the architecture of the room displays a beautifully vaulted room, suggests that Jung regarded the contribution of this period to the evolution of the psyche as a high-minded one. 'The beautifully vaulted room' reminds one, of course, of a church and that we are dealing with the historical period in which Christianity – Roman Catholicism – became dominant. Jung's father was a Christian minister and Jung was well aware of the influence of the spread of Christianity (Roman Catholicism) in this period. The fact that this floor is unfurnished and no artefacts are seen, unlike every other floor of the building, also suggests that the contribution of this period is a non-materialistic one.

In the final sequence of the dream, Jung discovers a stone slab with a ring in the floor, that can be pulled up to reveal 'a narrow stone stairway' leading down to a low cave cut into the rock. This part of the building corresponds to prehistoric times. Jung has described the cave as looking rather like a 'prehistoric grave' and such graves are, of course, one of our chief sources of knowledge of those times. In the dream, Jung sees two half-disintegrated human skulls and scattered bones in the thick dust of the grave, together with the remains of broken pottery. (Pottery vessels containing supplies for the journey into the next world often accompanied ancient burials.) This last floor of the house is in fact an underground stone cave, so that it is the only floor of the house that is not man-made, suggesting that the psyche of primitive man is as nature constructed it – largely uninfluenced by 'historical assumptions'.

From this analysis of the dream it is clearly apparent that Jung's dream was not an intimation from a wise unconscious of the hitherto undiscovered existence of the 'collective unconscious'. It was simply a metaphorical representation of the question which Jung was introspectively exploring when awake, namely the relationship between personal psychology and history. Jung's interpretation of the dream arises because he hasn't realised that the dream is a metaphorical representation of the relationship between two variables: history and psychology. By focusing on only one variable, namely the psyche, Jung almost inevitably concluded that the other variable (history) was the answer. In his own words, "my dream was giving me the answer", by showing him the many levels of historical consciousness (ie the collective unconscious) still operating beneath the individual's personal consciousness.

Ironically, in a contribution to a book made just before he died (Jung et al 1968) he offered a different explanation for the dream, this time focusing on the other variable in the dream – history. He now said he saw the dream as representing a history of his intellectual development, the tomb with the skulls and bones corresponding to his paleological interests, the ground floor dating from the Middle Ages corresponding to the influence of his parents' "mediaeval concepts" and the first floor corresponding to more recent intellectual influences. This analysis, however, misses out the basement dating from Roman times.

If Jung had related his first analysis based on the psyche and his second analysis which focused on historical development to the question he had been introspectively exploring prior to the dream, namely the relationship between these two variables, then the analysis might have turned out rather differently. It might have shown, as our analysis has, that his dream was an analogical representation of his waking introspections concerning the relationship between personal psychology and history.

We can now see the reason why the patients of Jungian analysts tend to dream dreams that appear to confirm Jungian theory while the patients of Freudian analysts tend to dream dreams that confirm Freudian theory. The subject matter of dreams are emotionally arousing introspections that remain unmanifested in the external world. Patients will introspect about their problems in terms of the theoretical framework in which the therapist sets them. This theoretical framework will be represented metaphorically or symbolically in the patient's dreams. The analyst then takes this symbolical representation of his own theory as evidence for the correctness of that theory. In just this way Jung, introspecting about the possible relationship between the psyche and history, had a dream in which those waking thoughts were metaphorically represented and then put forward the dream images as evidence for the veracity of that same speculation. This position is not too dissimilar to a person who has a certain theory about human nature and then commissions the making of a film in which people act out his ideas. Subsequently, forgetting the origin of his film, he offers the same film as independent evidence for the correctness of his theory.

I would suggest this mistaken pattern of dream interpretation could also lead to false memories of abuse. Suppose a client goes to see a therapist with certain symptoms such as an eating disorder for example. If the therapist believed the commonly held, but scientifically unsupported, view that eating disorders are most frequently caused by sexual abuse in childhood then the therapist might convey this belief to the client. Even if the client has no conscious memories of such abuse she'll still naturally introspect about this emotionally charged suggestion which in turn will give rise to metaphorical dreams about abuse. If the client reports these dreams to the therapist, the therapist may well interpret them as providing independent evidence of the abuse having taken place. A mistake with potentially tragic consequences as the client can come to believe that the imagined abuse did take place.

Chapter 7

CREATIVITY AND DREAMS

Solving problems

THE RELATIONSHIP between creativity and dreams has long been a matter for speculation. There are many recorded anecdotes of dreams helping people solve problems. My research into the origin of why we dream is a case in point. It was inspired by a dream. That dream eventually led to this new theory.

The dream occurred after I had abandoned earlier attempts to explain the origin of dreams when I could see no meaningful way to integrate the cross species REM findings and the apparent complexity of human dreaming. I suddenly perceived the relationship between my own dream one morning and my waking introspections of a few moments earlier (see Dream 1). This suggested to me that there might be a lawful relationship between waking experience and dreaming and that, for some as yet unexplained reason, symbolism or metaphor might be the form in which that relationship *had* to be expressed. It took a further ten years of research before the integration of these factors evolved and the reason became clear enough to be presentable in book form.

That dream, however, is not directly comparable to dreams which apparently give rise to the solutions of problems because in the latter kind of dreams the actual dream content has a direct relationship with the problem being solved. Take, for example, in this regard, one of the most famous dream anecdotes of all: Kekule's discovery of the structure of the benzene ring, one of the most important discoveries in the history of chemistry. He had been trying for years to solve the problem of the molecular structure of benzene.

Kekule's dream

> Then, one afternoon, I turned my chair to the fire
> and dozed. Again the atoms were gambolling before
> my eyes. This time the smaller groups kept modestly
> in the background. My mental eye, rendered more
> acute by repeated visions of this kind, could now
> distinguish larger structures of manifold con-
> formation: long rows, sometimes more closely fitted
> together, all twining and twisting in a snake like
> motion. But look! What was this? One of the snakes
> had seized hold of its own tail, and the forms whirled
> mockingly before my eyes. As if by a flash of
> lightening I awoke .... Let us learn to dream
> gentlemen. (Arthur Koestler, *The Act of Creation.*)

The snake swallowing its own tail suggested to Kekule
that the structure of this organic compound might be a
closed ring. Would we be right in concluding from this
that the dream solved the problem for Kekule which his
waking conscious mind could not?

My theory suggests an interpretation of the events of
the dream as follows: Kekule had worked hard on the
problem trying out many different solutions but without
success. He feels he is getting nowhere. He sits by the
fire and starts to doze. The dream which follows expresses
his frustration concerning the problem. He sees the
'manifold confor-mation: long rows, sometimes more
closely fitted together', that is, the numerous solutions
he had tried, some more closely fitting the solution than
others 'all twining and twisting in snake-like fashion' –
this suggests his continuing attempts to fashion or model
the correct shape of the structure. 'What was this? One
of the snakes had seized hold of its own tail, and the
forms whirled mockingly before my eyes' – we see here an
analogical expression of Kekule's frustration. His attempts
at a solution are just going around in circles. The problem
is making a fool of him, ie mocking him.

This interpretation is given further credence by the fact that Kekule's dream occurs just after nodding off to sleep. This stage of sleep is not REM sleep but that drowsy state called 'hypnagogic sleep'. The E.E.G. brain wave pattern is similar to REM sleep, although the lower brainstem is not as involved as it is in REM sleep proper. We have seen with Silberer's research that a current waking introspection may get translated into a sensory analogue during hypnagogic sleep. Similarly, we would expect Kekule's dream to reflect his waking frustration at the lack of progress in his attempts to solve his problem. This is exactly what my dream analysis shows did in fact happen.

Although the dream represents Kekule's frustration at not being able to find the correct solution to the problem, the image in the dream of going around in circles breaks him free from his mental set of looking for a linear solution to the problem and opens the possibility that a circular structure might provide the solution. Are we to assume then that it was pure coincidence that led to the selection of the image of the whirling circle to represent the feelings of frustration? Research by Dement (1972) suggests an answer to this problem, but first we must consider how the creative process works.

Stages in the creative process

In 1926 Wallace, in *The Art of Thought*, concisely described the stages in the creative process. They are: preparation, incubation, illumination and verification.

We have all had experience of working on a problem (preparation), then leaving the problem aside, perhaps going for a walk (incubation), then suddenly a solution hits us (illumination) and, of course, we have to check the solution (verification). The characteristic mode of functioning of the cognitive unconscious which 'incubates' the problem, is nature's way of allowing us a holistic approach to it. The solution doesn't come from a logical analysis, although such an analysis is necessary in the preparatory stage, but in rearranging the elements of the problem into a new pattern or seeing the existing pattern from a different perspective.

You can see the process clearly at work if you apply the theory of dreams presented in this book to your own dreams. First you note all the elements of the dream, including your feelings about it. These are the feelings that you would have felt had you been able to enact out the waking introspections that gave rise to your dreams. The feelings in the dream are actually more intense than the feelings you had when you were awake, as you did not act on the feelings when you were awake. Next, compare the dream elements to your waking experience of the previous day to see if you can find a matching template to the dream scenario. Remembering of course that the match will not be between the 'objective' waking events and the dream but rather between the dream and your introspected view of those waking events. This can be regarded as the preparation phase of the dream analysis.

The corresponding waking situation doesn't usually spring to mind immediately. This is because the purpose of the dream in the first instance is to deactivate that memory. Hence it usually requires a period of 'incubation' before the unconscious mind can reactivate it. Presumably a number of associative links to the waking introspection have to be traced before the waking memory on which the dream is based can be reactivated. In fact, many studies show that there *is* a connection between REM sleep and the effectiveness of memory recall for new learning. This is especially so for those types of learning that involve 'false starts', such as procedural memory as demonstrated by Professor Peretz Lavie in learning the path through a maze (Lavie, 1994). My theory suggests that the reason for this is that the REM sleep allows the introspected false starts that were not acted upon to be deactivated. With the autonomic arousal switched off following the analogical acting out of the introspected false starts, the 'correct' memory can then be consolidated and hence the improvement in memory for certain types of learning following REM sleep.

Professor Lavie even speculated on whether or not we need REM sleep at all on the basis of a patient he discovered who has little or no REM sleep. This patient was injured in the Arab-Israeli war and was found to have a piece of shrapnel lodged in his brainstem in the same spot that Jouvet discovered was responsible for triggering REM sleep. Professor Francis Crick, the Nobel prize winner whose 'dream to forget' theory is described in chapter 3, was taken aback by this finding. He urged Professor Lavie to do further extensive tests to discover if there might not be some subtle malfunction of the patient's memory. But, in spite of extensive observations, Professor Lavie could find no malfunction in the patient's memory or thinking. The patient had developed a successful law practice and was also particularly adept at doing crossword puzzles. From the perspective of my theory this finding is not anomalous but would in fact be predicted.

The onset of REM sleep is controlled by the acetylcholine neurons in the brainstem. These cells also trigger the orientation response which activates the flight or fight readiness in the muscles. (The flight or fight mechanism is the part of our nervous system which prepares us to react to an emergency.) It is this activation of the flight or fight response accompanying certain introspections that I believe gives rise to dreams. If this mechanism is deactivated, not only will there be no dreams, there will be no need for them. Instead of looking for cognitive or memory impairment Professors Lavie and Crick might have had more revealing results by checking to see if this patient was capable of responding with arousal to novel stimuli. The deactivation of the flight or fight mechanism would make such a response unlikely. The absence of this process would impair performance on those occasions when instant reactions are required to novel stimuli, for example, when driving. I would also expect this patient to be an emotionally cool person, perhaps the kind of person who would find crossword puzzles a compelling activity.

The incubation period of the creative process may take years because the illumination stage is awaiting a vital piece of missing information. Such was the case with the development of my analogical theory of dreams. After making the discovery that dreams are based on emotionally arousing introspections, I observed that these introspections are expressed in sensory scenarios, but that the original images are always replaced by related images in the dream scenario. It was as if the brain was somehow inhibited from using the original images and had to use related images instead. But this raised two further questions. Firstly, what purpose was served by the replacement of the original images? Secondly, why does the brain not use the original images? The most likely purpose seemed to be that dreams discharged the arousal caused by the unmanifested introspections. Indeed there was substantial evidence, as reviewed in the chapter on biology, that this was so. But there was a difficulty with this explanation as was pointed out to me by Dr A Mayes of Manchester University: why should using analogically related images deactivate the unmanifested emotionally arousing introspections?

After some considerable time thinking about this, it

suddenly occurred to me that instinctive knowledge would have to be programmed in an incomplete way to allow for environmental variation. For example, the genetic description of its species programmed into a duck's brain has to be sufficiently flexible or indeterminate to include all the possible variations found within the duck species. In other words the genetic description will have to be along the lines of "here are some of the parameters, find something that corresponds to this". The same form of processing used in the REM state for programming instincts, if applied to introspections, would result in memory going on a search for related images in which to express these introspections. The brain would then react to the newly found related images as if they were the real thing. And thus the related dream images would deactivate the emotional arousal of the autonomic nervous system caused by unresolved worries while awake.

The difficulty I found with this explanation was that it seemed to push the original reason for why we dream way back into evolutionary history. But we still have dreams. Intuitively I felt that, for the explanation to be satisfying, it should relate to the reality of the human species as it is today, not just be something left over from what may have been necessary hundreds of millions of years ago in our evolutionary history. So I put this explanation on the shelf and continued to search for a more satisfying answer.

Then, one rainy day, I happened to pick up a copy of Robert Ornstein's *The Psychology of Consciousness*. In it I came across a list of right brain/left brain functions and the dichotomy of 'rationalisation versus metaphoric' (logical thought versus analogical thought) leaped out from the page. I saw at once that what I had observed taking place in dreams was a metaphorical or analogical translation of waking introspections. The right cortex in humans is specialised for the perception and under-standing of metaphor. The more I read about metaphorical thinking the more clear it became that metaphorical thinking was central to the way our brains function. Even language itself can be seen as the acquisition of a social analogue for an instinctive knowledge – the deep structure of language.

Now the explanation as to why dreams were expressed in related images no longer applied just to our evolutionary history but was central to the way our minds develop and function today. It suddenly seemed obvious that we could not have flexibility of human behaviour without a flexible and sophisticated analogical thinking process through which instinctive knowledge is expressed. In fact, the less specified the instinctive orientation the more scope there is for us to adapt rapidly to changing circumstances. Our flexible analogical thought processes allow us to more easily generate a range of environmental analogues to adapt our instinctive orientations to a changing environment.

Now that I had recognised that the process I had observed in dreams was a metaphorical or analogical translation, this was no longer a remote evolutionary process but one that was central to the organisation and expression of the human mind. Thus we can see that the 'incubation' process may extend over many years until missing pieces of information fall into place and the process is complete.

Dreams, then, deactivate emotional arousal associated with waking introspections by acting them out in sensory analogues. This naturally makes it more difficult to recall the original waking experience since, once it is translated into, and acted out as, a sensory analogue, it no longer possesses an emotional charge. The memory is therefore not accessible to a reductionist analysis of the manifest content such as Freud undertook. This may be why Freud missed seeing the metaphorical parallel between his dream of 'Irma's injection' and the events of the 'Emma Eckstein' case.

Following the preparatory phase of examining the manifest content, a period of waiting or 'incubation' is required whilst our metaphorical right brain goes on a search for the matching template from earlier events when we were awake. Of course, examining the manifest content will provide clues to guide that search.

The feelings expressed in the dream are also vital clues. Knowing that the characters and actions in the dream are actually in an analogous relationship to a waking introspection from yesterday is what primes the unconscious search for the matching template from our previous day's waking experience. This search may be further helped if, from time to time, we re-examine the elements in the manifest content. When a possible match between the dream and a waking introspection occurs to us – 'illumination' – then we enter the 'verification' phase. We check out the match between our dream and the waking template. Do the feelings match (remembering that the feelings will be much more 'real' in the dream because they appear to be occurring in reality rather than fantasy)? Do the characters match? Does the action sequence match?

Ironically it is often easier, provided we have adequate background information, to see the meaning of someone else's dream. This is because the waking sequence has not been deactivated in *our* brains. Thus my wife, Liz, will often identify the meaning of one of my dreams before I do and vice versa. Real dream interpretation, especially interpreting our own dreams, clearly involves the four traditional phases of creative problem solving, namely, preparation, incubation, illumination and verification.

Despite popular ideas to the contrary it appears that successful problem solving in dreams may be pretty rare. In 1972 Dement reports a study in which five hundred undergraduate students, over three consecutive classes, were given one of three problems to solve. They were told to study a problem for fifteen minutes before going to sleep and to record any dreams remembered in the night. If the problem had not been solved, they were to work on it for another fifteen minutes in the morning. The total number of problem solving attempts was one thousand one hundred and forty eight. It was judged that eighty seven dreams related to the problem but that the problem was solved in a dream on only seven occasions.

One of the problems was as follows: "The letters OTTFF... form the beginning of an infinite sequence. Find a simple rule for determining any or all successive letters. According to your rule, what would be the next two letters of the sequence?" The next two letters are SS. The letters represent the first letters used in spelling out the numerical sequence one, two, three, four, five, six, seven etc.

The following dream is one of those in which the problem was solved.

The art gallery

I was standing in an art gallery looking at the paintings on the wall. As I walked down the hall, I began to count the paintings one, two three, four, five. But as I came to the sixth and seventh, the paintings had been ripped from their frames! I stared at the empty frames with a peculiar feeling that some mystery was about to suddenly be solved, I realised that the sixth and seventh spaces were the solution to the problem.

A second problem the students were given was to consider

the letters HIJKLMNO. The solution to the problem was one word: water. In other words, H to O or H_2O.

No dream was classified as actually solving the problem, but twelve were classified as 'mode of expression dreams'. An example of a 'mode of expression' dream is as follows: "I had several dreams, all of which had water in them somewhere. In one dream I was hunting for sharks. In another I was riding waves at the ocean. In another I was confronted by a barracuda while skin-diving. In another it was raining quite heavily. In another I was sailing into the wind." This student had solved the problem to his own satisfaction before going to bed, with the word 'alphabet'.

The type of holistic thinking required for creative problem solving is the antithesis of the everyday analytical approach. Rather than breaking a problem down, it involves looking at the entire problem from a different perspective. This is also the type of thinking required to solve the problems in Dement's study. Such creative problem solving is often facilitated by taking a break from the problem and getting into a relaxed frame of mind (incubation) and then the solution often 'hits' us. It may well be that the dream can, in a sense, provide the relaxed frame of mind in which a solution can emerge. An individual's analogical thinking process may have arrived at a solution before dreaming, but he is either too tired or, more likely, too set in an analytical mode of thinking, for the solution to emerge.

In 1981 Dixon reported experiments where a subliminal image shown to subjects appeared in the manifest content of a subsequent dream. He argued that in these cases the stimulus doesn't possess enough energy to get as far as waking consciousness so it emerges in the less controlled consciousness of the dream. Perhaps a similar phenomenon exists as far as dream problem solving is concerned. A solution that doesn't possess enough energy to break through into consciousness, either because of existing cognitive sets being too rigid or because the person is not in a suitably relaxed frame of mind, may become manifest in a dream sequence.

How the solution manifests depends on how the person anticipates what will happen in his or her dream. In the first example given, the subject has the solution expressed clearly in an analogous setting. He is looking at paintings in an art gallery. This is an analogy for his anticipation of looking at images in a dream. The sixth and seventh paintings, ripped from their frames, symbolised the missing two letters which had to be found in order to solve the problem. He *expects* the problem to be solved in a dream. He looks at the blank paintings with a feeling that some mystery is going to be solved. He realises that the sixth and seventh spaces are the solution.

This dream, then, is an analogical representation of what this student *anticipated* would happen in a dream that night. This student's analogical thinking process had probably arrived at a correct solution before the dream occurred. Consequently the anticipated solution provided in the dream was an accurate analogy of the correct solution. This is in contrast to the great majority of dreams reported which concerned the problem but in which the correct solution did not emerge.

In the second example, the student wrongly thought that he had solved the problem before going to sleep. In that case, my theory of dreams would lead us to expect that, for the solution to appear in the dream, it would have to be incorporated into the ongoing imagery of other dream themes since he no longer anticipated a solution in his dream. This would be similar to the subliminally presented images previously mentioned which were incorporated into the ongoing dream sequences. This student reported several dreams in which water was the main symbolism. However, the dreams were not about the problem, or about water as the solution to the problem, but rather water as a symbol to express a personal concern for the future, a fear that he was heading into 'dangerous waters'.

This student's analogical thinking process had arrived at the correct solution, namely 'water', but, because he wrongly believed 'alphabet' was the solution, it did not emerge into waking consciousness and, like a subliminally presented stimulus, was easily incorporated into the symbolism or analogies in his dreams that were expressing a different waking anticipation.

Similarly with Kekule's dream. I will suggest that his analogical thinking process had arrived at a correct solution but a suitable frame of mind for its emergence may not have arrived before Kekule fell asleep or else his conscious mental sets were too rigid to permit the solution to emerge. So the solution was favourably disposed to be incorporated into the symbolism or analogy in a dream, expressing some waking anticipation. In this case Kekule's fear that the problem was making a fool of him is expressed appropriately by the snake chasing its own tail, 'mockingly' going round in circles. My theory will suggest that, for a problem to be directly solved in a dream, the dreamer must actively anticipate that the problem will be solved in the dream and, secondly, the correct solution must have already occurred to him prior to the dream. On the other hand, where a solution has occurred to a person's unconscious mind, but an appropriate milieu for its expression has not been found while they were awake, then the solution may be indirectly suggested by the surface imagery of the metaphor expressing a waking concern – as in the examples of Kekule's dream and in the water solution dream just described.

To further demonstrate these two modes of problem solving by means of dreams, I will first consider a follow up to Dement's research that illustrates the first mode and then describe how two inventions, lead shot and the automatic sewing machine, illustrate the second mode.

The interesting follow up to Dement's research is described by Brian Inglis in his book *The Power of Dreams* (1987). The *New Scientist* asked its readers to use their dreams to solve a number of intellectual problems. They were the kind of problems that would be expected to baffle the logical, conscious mind. Eleven people wrote to Morton Schatzman, who was conducting the research, and described how a dream had helped them solve the following mathematical problem:

Using six line segments of equal length can you construct four equilateral triangles such that the sides of the triangles are the same length as the line segments.

Eleven people wrote in saying that a dream had helped them to solve the problem. A student wrote saying that in a dream she ran her hand along some railings when six of them came together "to form a kind of wigwam". Later she dreamt that her chemistry teacher appeared in the dream and said '109 28'. The student knew this number was connected with tetrahedral molecules whose structures makes up four equilateral triangles. Translating the metaphor she realised that the solution was a three sided-pyramid. Another student who was not familiar with mathematics was delighted with the help her dream provided. In her dream she asked a scientist for help and the scientist jumped up and down, and eventually flew up on top of a cupboard. When the dreamer woke up, she was able to understand the metaphorical answer by realising that the triangles must be given lift-off. She made a drawing using this idea and solved the problem.

Notice how the presence of the scientist in the dream would naturally alert her waking mind to the fact that this dream was about the problem from the *New Scientist* magazine.

Another problem presented was to discover what was remarkable about the following sentence:

I am not very happy acting pleased whenever prominent scientists overmagnify intellectual enlightenment.

The number of letters increases in each consecutive word by one to form a numerical sequence going from one to thirteen.

One sixth-form student dreamed that he was lecturing to scientists seated at five tables with one, two, three, four and five, scientists sitting at each respective table. The student was able to see that the dream was a metaphorical solution to the problem. Another student who solved the problem by means of a dream reported that in his dream he typed the sentence 'the quick brown fox jumped over the lazy dog'. (This is, of course, the sentence that contains all twenty six letters of the alphabet.) His supervisor tells him to type 1 2 3 4 5 6 7 8 9 instead. Again we see the dream expressing the solution metaphorically. The words were replaced by a sentence known to contain all the letters of the alphabet, and thus it directs his attention to the letters in the words. The supervisor tells him to write a sequence of numbers that stops at 9. This is because the number of words in the replacement sentence in the dream has nine words in it unlike the problem sentence which has thirteen words in it. We can see that the dream is providing an analogical solution to the problem.

In these examples the dreamers were anticipating a solution to the problem in their dreams and then dream a metaphorical solution to the problem. In the next two examples a solution to the problem is not being anticipated in a dream and so the solution has to follow the more indirect route of being incorporated into the surface images of a dream expressing another theme.

Invention and dreams

The making of lead shot is another example of a dream solution becoming incorporated into the surface structure of a metaphor expressing an ongoing concern of a dreamer. In 1782 William Watts invented the process that enabled lead shot to be made in regular shapes and sizes. One night, coming home from a drinking session, he decided to sleep it off in the porch of the church near his home. During the night it rained heavily and he had a dream. He dreamed that his wife was pouring drops of molten lead on top of him from the roof of the church. No doubt he was apprehensive of the scalding his wife would give him when he got home, and this provided the metaphor of his wife (who is not actually seen in the dream) expressing her hostility by pouring molten lead on him. In other words, his dream expressed the feeling that he would get 'shot' when his wife got her hands on him.

Watts was a plumber who was well used to working with lead and familiar with the way molten lead behaves. He was also aware of the problems in making lead shot and I will suggest his unconscious must have already solved the problem before he had the dream. He already knew that molten lead dropped through the air would form perfect spherical lead balls. Although the solution had 'incubated', the 'illumination' had yet to take place. The solution is incorporated into the surface structure of the dream metaphor. This again is a similar process to the subliminal stimulus being incorporated into the surface structure of the dream metaphor.

When Watts woke up he immediately saw that he had a means of making lead shot of a regular shape and size.

He carried out an experiment to test the illumination. With the help of his wife (who had presumably cooled down by now) he dropped molten lead from a considerable height – actually from the church roof – and it did indeed form perfect lead shot as it fell through the air and cooled. This process is used to this day to make lead shot.

A further example is the invention, in 1846, of the first practical sewing machine. For years an inventor called Elias Howe had been trying to build a sewing machine but, like everyone else who was trying to do the same thing at that time, he couldn't make his designs work. But he was desperate to succeed because he was being hard pressed for money by his creditors. A solution eluded him and his struggle seemed fruitless. Then, one night, he dreamed that he was chased and captured by a savage tribe who told him they would spear him to death within twenty four hours if he didn't solve the problem. They tied him to a stake and began wildly dancing round him, waving their spears and getting closer all the time. As they got closer and closer he got more and more desperate and, when they seemed on the point of killing him, he suddenly noticed that their spears all had an eye hole near the point. He woke with a start, remembered the dream, and realised at once that this was the solution to his problem. The eye in the needle needed to be on the opposite end to a hand-held needle. The model of the hand-held needle may have conditioned his conscious mind making it difficult for him to see that the functional elements of a needle would have to be rearranged if the needle was to work on a sewing machine.

The solution 'hitched a ride' up to consciousness, as it were, by being incorporated into the surface imagery of the dream metaphor that was expressing his frustration at being pressurised by his creditors (savages in the dream). This dream changed the working lives of millions.

The evidence, therefore, suggests that there are two possible ways that dreams may provide solutions to problems. Firstly, if a person has worked on a problem for which he has not found a solution, then goes to bed expecting to dream one, he may just dream a metaphorical solution. However, this requires (a) that he has an emotionally arousing expectation that the solution to the problem will be revealed in a dream, (b) that his unconscious reaches a solution to the problem before he dreams, (c) that the solution does not reach consciousness before dreaming, and (d) that he recalls the dream in which the solution appears. This can only work for a short time. As soon as the subject has experienced *not* dreaming the correct solution (which is bound to happen sooner or later) then he will no longer be able to generate the necessary emotionally arousing expectation that his dream is going to provide the answer.

A second and perhaps more likely possibility is that the surface structure of a dream whose metaphorical content expresses a particular waking concern may, on occasion, provide the vehicle to express the solution to a particular problem. But this would only occur when the unconscious mind has incubated a solution and is looking for an opportunity to express it – as with the discovery of the 'benzene ring' and the invention of the sewing machine.

So dreams in which problems are solved do not present a difficulty for this new theory of dreams. Indeed, such solutions emerge in a form that is in accordance with what the theory would predict.

Chapter 8

THE METAPHORICAL MIND

Applications of the theory

I HAVE presented evidence in this book that dreams are an analogical or metaphorical acting out of introspections from the previous day, where autonomic nervous system arousal was stimulated by the introspection but not discharged.

I have also shown that metaphorical communication is an intrinsic part of the way we understand and communicate our experience. Such metaphorical expression as is found in dreams may also be more widespread in waking life than is generally realised. A sudden burst of song, for example, is often a metaphorical expression of how a person is feeling about a certain issue. A woman who didn't want to get pregnant, though her spouse wanted her to, was frequently heard to sing, 'what do you get when you fall in love, you get enough germs to fill an ocean, that's what you get for your devotion'. As a nurse, this lady was well aware that the average male ejaculation contains millions of sperm, ie "enough germs to fill an ocean".

A friend of mine was once worried about his job. When his wife read out a number of suitable job vacancies from the paper, he spontaneously sang: "Through the eyes of love you can see a thousand stars". There clearly appears to be a metaphorical connection between the stars and the job opportunities.

On another occasion I was congratulating a relative who had come to live with us on his new job when he suddenly burst into song: "what would you do if I sang out of tune, would you stand up and walk out on me". The song metaphorically expressed his worry as to how we might react towards him if his new job didn't work out.

Another friend, who was known to be worrying about his business overdraft, was frequently heard singing: "I've sold my soul to the company store".

Once you are sensitised to the prevalence of metaphor in our communications, you may be surprised to discover that an apparently irrelevant anecdote which a friend or relative suddenly feels inspired to tell may be an actual metaphor for how they feel about an aspect of your relationship with them, which they are consciously reluctant to communicate.

I recently conducted a weekend workshop at a small residential college. A couple I knew quite well were also spending the weekend at the college at the invitation of one of the workshop participants who lived in the college. As the weekend progressed it was evident that our mutual friends felt somewhat excluded from what was going on. Yet we felt it was inappropriate to invite them to participate in the workshop. At the end of the weekend I was speaking to one member of the couple when she suddenly felt impelled to tell me the following anecdote:

A metaphorical rebuke

> We recently visited some old friends, John and Julia Clare, whom we hadn't seen for some time. We hadn't been invited to see them, we just decided to call on the spur of the moment. But they were very cool. John said that he was expecting friends that had been invited. I didn't know why he should have treated us like this, especially when you consider how often he has visited us and brought his friends around to our house.

My friend looked at me intently as she told me this anecdote and seemed satisfied on noting my perplexity about why anyone should behave so unreasonably. Her anecdote is a perfect metaphorical description of her frustration at not being invited to participate in the workshop. It may well be that this unconscious communication of her frustration at being excluded from the weekend workshop obviated the need for her to have a dream that night to deactivate the activated intro-spection underlying her frustration.

We commonly use metaphors to explain to someone else something they have not had an experience of. I recently went out with a friend to dinner at a restaurant which neither of us had been to before. Whilst we waited for our table we were given the menu to study. Ostrich meat was one of the dishes on offer that night. Neither I nor my friend had ever eaten it and we speculated out loud about whether we would try it. Another customer who was also waiting for a table said, "I've tried it. It's a very interesting dish". I asked him what it tasted like and after a moment's thought he said, "well, it has the texture of liver and it tastes like venison ought to taste like." When we ate the ostrich meat a little later, we both agreed that the analogy he had given for what ostrich meat might taste like was very accurate indeed. It really did have a texture like liver and a more gamy flavour than one usually associates with venison.

Even young children have the ability to use metaphor and analogy creatively. Recently at breakfast my four year old daughter asked for a glass of milk. After a few sips she put the glass down and started to leave the table. I looked at her rather sternly, since she has the inclination, if allowed, to eat only a little at meal times but then declare an hour later that she is hungry again. Seeing my stern look she said calmly, "Daddy, doesn't Mammy sometimes make you a cup of tea, and you don't drink it all?" I had to admit to myself this is something that happens not infrequently. Liz gives me a cup of tea and, after a couple of sips, I get engrossed in what I am reading or writing and forget all about the tea. In all honesty I could not deny that her analogy was accurate and consequently said nothing as she imperiously got down from the table with her milk unfinished.

Just as we have the potential to identify appropriate metaphors we can also, of course, make inappropriate matches between two patterns. In fact my theory implies that this is inevitably going to happen on some occasions. Remember that the capacity for analogy or metaphor derives from the programming of instinctive behaviour. The instinctive templates only partly specify the pattern to be identified in order to allow for flexibility of response to animals' individual environments.

Many people may recall the pictures of ethologist Konrad Lorenz (1962) being followed by a family of young goslings. It seems that goslings are preprogrammed to become attached to the first moving object they encounter after hatching. The programmed rule seems to be something like "when you get out of your shell your mother is the first large moving object you see". Now, if that large moving object is Konrad Lorenz, clearly the wrong patterns have been identified. The birds bonded with Lorenz, they followed him persistently, they became distressed when he left them and ran to him for support when they felt frightened. Clearly this is a situation where the matching of an instinctive template to its environmental counterpart has gone awry and humans are not immune from something similar.

Human beings, as I have pointed out many times in this book, have a special capacity for identifying metaphor and such a capacity is vital for allowing our instinctive influences to be flexibly applied in our environments, ie to match instinctive templates to environmental contingencies. We have this ability to think logically, to break problems down and analyse them. We also have the ability to think analogically, that is, to think holistically and to recognise how a pattern matches another pattern. Our conscious mind's preferred mode of action is logical thought whilst our unconscious mind's preferred mode is analogical thought, or 'association of ideas, as it is sometimes called. I think that a great many mental problems may be caused by this emotional process going awry and that it is central to good psychotherapeutic practise for psychotherapists to be aware of this process.

Implications for psychotherapy

Let me illustrate with a personal experience how the metaphorical process can lead to mental problems. Our television set broke down. It is a large TV and Liz and I held an end each and carried it through the main square of the town to the repair shop. Suddenly I felt acutely self conscious. I felt as though people knew something intimate and embarrassing about our domestic situation. Driving back to our home having delivered the television set to the repair shop, I found myself making very negative comments about life. I found myself saying: "maybe it would have been better not to have been born, then one wouldn't have to go through all this hassle". I felt surprise at myself for saying this.

A little while later sitting at home I found myself feeling depressed. This had nothing directly to do with the absence of the television since I was looking forward to having a break from it. The feeling of depression was very real. I asked myself where this was coming from. I reflected that my circumstances were as good now as they had ever been, so I focused on the feeling of depression for a moment to see what might be recalled.

I found myself back in a memory of childhood when I was fourteen years old, escorting my mother through the local town to the doctors surgery. My mother needed assistance since she had difficulty keeping her balance. She also appeared to be in disturbingly and uncharacteristically flippant mood. She had been in this childish laughing and girlish mood ever since she had taken medicine prescribed by the doctor to relieve her menopausal symptoms. The doctor was to say when we met him a little later: "Mrs Griffin, you're drunk!" My mother, who rarely drank alcohol, had reacted to the alcohol content of the medicine by becoming inebriated.

As I held her arm walking down that high street, I felt acutely self conscious. It seemed as though my very survival depended on none of my school mates seeing us. It would be bad enough to be seen holding your mothers arm going down the street but for my mother to be giggling and staggering as well would have meant endless ridicule. I was also aware that I was totally without control over the outcome. I couldn't abandon my mother. I would actually have to walk past the top of the very road that led up to the school.

Young men are acutely aware of the need for peer approval and compete for individual status in the peer group. During our teenage years we seem to be especially aware of the need to maintain peer group acceptability whilst struggling to find our sense of identity. In the wild, animals that have been rejected by their social group are in a dangerous situation and their very survival may be at stake. We could certainly expect an instinctive recognition on the part of most young men to the danger of peer group rejection. The feelings I had as I escorted my 'inebriated' mother to the doctor were entirely appropriate. But to feel the same way as I accompanied my wife Liz with a broken-down television set, up a side street, from the main square of a different town more than thirty years later is hardly appropriate. We can see this situation as a mismatch of templates. Yes, the patterns have some elements in common but a television set with a problem is not the same as a mother with a problem and a middle aged man is not the same as a young man.

The consequences of this mismatch were a sudden feeling of hopelessness, which released a cascade of organic compounds that prolonged the depressed state. Having identified the mismatch of templates and reflected on how well my life was going, it still took about an hour to shake off the depressed state. What if I had continued to think negative thoughts and prolonged that depressed state? What if I had then gone to a therapist inclined to explore my past while I was in that state of mind? I would be looking for everything that had ever gone wrong in my life. Clearly such a psychotherapeutic process would reinforce the depressive state rather than extinguish it.

To take another example, suppose a woman had been sexually abused when she was young and now finds she is having difficulty in her new relationship even though she loves her partner. What may be happening is that she is wrongly identifying sex with her partner now as being similar to the experience of sexual abuse she was subjected to when she was a child. Consciously she may know the two situations are different, but her metaphorical mind has made the connection and is not letting it go. In this situation a therapist with a psychodynamic perspective might encourage this woman to get in touch with her past feelings of abuse and to explore her childhood memories of abuse in great detail. The danger here is that such an exploration will give the 'abuse' template even greater prominence and exacerbate the problem even further.

An able therapist, by contrast, would help the client to reframe the abuse situation, putting new perspectives on the abuse so the client can distance herself from the traumatic memories, place a boundary around them and thus to limit the influence of the past abuse on her life today. (One very helpful way of doing this is to encourage the abused person to see more clearly that her present relationship is not analogous to the past abuse situation. The client, for example, could be asked to list a hundred ways her new relationship differs from the abusive relationship. This exercise helps the client to uncouple the mismatched templates.)

The failure to recognise that emotional problems often occur because of this mismatch of past and present experiences, ie because of the perception of false analogies, has in my opinion held back the development and the acceptance of effective psychotherapeutic approaches.

Conversely, the ability to perceive analogies and metaphor can have a positive contribution to make to psychotherapy. This has always been appreciated by the traditional psychologies of the east.

The use of metaphor in teaching stories was brought to perfection as a communication instrument many thousands of years ago. As part of ancient teaching traditions such stories have highly sophisticated, multiple levels of meaning and were deliberately designed to bypass the limitations of the conditioned mind in order to allow a more objective assessment of the message contained in the story (Shah, 1964, 1968). The messages in the stories are like blueprints stored in the mind, waiting for the appropriate moment when they enable you to see a pattern in events which you hadn't seen before, thus deepening the understanding of those events.

A well-known example of such a teaching story is the Sufi tale of the village where all the residents were blind, and an elephant, a creature unknown in those parts, had wandered into the village. The villagers, anxious to know what it was, appointed a committee to examine it and report back. But, as they did not know the form or shape of the elephant, they groped sightlessly, gathering some information by touching some part of it. When the committee returned, the other villagers gathered round – each of them anxious, misguidedly, to learn the truth from those who were themselves astray. They listened to all they were told. One man who had touched one of the elephant's legs declared that it was firm, like a pillar. Another who had managed to reach up to an ear said it was like a rough carpet. A third had felt the swish of its tail and said it was a moving brush whilst another who had felt its trunk argued that it was some kind of reptile. Each of the blind investigators perceived it wrongly. Each was convinced he was right.

This story, on one level, beautifully illustrates and brings home to us the fallacy of jumping to conclusions from inadequate data. It does so in a way that the ordinary intellect using language could never do.

The increasing use of metaphor in psychotherapy owes much to the work of the late Dr. Milton Erickson, the American psychiatrist, now generally acknowledged as the most effective psychotherapist of his generation. He showed that appropriate metaphors can bypass the limitations of conscious mental sets and mobilise the resources of the unconscious mind for therapeutic change. (Erickson, 1980, Rosen, 1982).

Dreams and psychotherapy

The dream which a patient brings to a therapist may be a powerful metaphorical statement of how the patient sees himself, his problem or his relationship to the therapist. Three dreams which were told to me during a psychotherapy workshop illustrate this point. Participants were asked if they had any dreams that they would like help in understanding. The first dream offered is as follows:

The monster fish

> I'm walking along a beach accompanied by a man I
> know, although I didn't see his face. There are
> twenty-first century buildings along the beach.
> Although somewhat fearful, I accompany the man
> into the sea for a swim. Our movements stir up a lot
> of muddy water, which arouses a monstrous fish
> which chases us. The fish follows us into a twenty-
> first century building, where, to the relief of both of
> us, the man stabs it to death with a knife.

The dreamer knew the dream was significant but felt
alienated from the meaning offered by her therapist who
had explained that the monster represented her emotional
self which didn't want to make decisions and the man
represented the decisive part of her which the dream
showed was now taking charge. But the dreamer herself,
felt that she would want to understand the emotional
side of herself – not kill it. She also mentioned that her
therapist belonged to a school of psychotherapy that
regards itself as taking the supposed insights of Freud
and Jung a major step further.

Although it is not possible to be entirely certain what
the dream means, it seems likely that the dream is a
metaphorical reflection of the dreamer's introspection
concerning her therapy. The twenty-first century buildings
reflect the ideological belief that her therapy is a more
evolved form than other current forms of psychotherapy
– the idea her therapist put forward. The man
accompanying her probably stands in for her therapist.
The swim in the sea – stirring up muddy water – refers to
her therapy and the investigation of "not pleasant"
experiences in her past which she said took place during
the sessions with her therapist. The monstrous fish is a
metaphor or symbol for what might be uncovered during
this investigation of her murky past – stirring up the dirty

water. The fact that the man kills the monstrous fish in the twenty-first century building reflects her belief that this futuristic psychotherapy would be able to get rid of any emotional monsters that might be released.

The dreamer, on hearing this explanation, felt that it intuitively made sense, and was much relieved. Had her therapist been able to correctly interpret her dream she would have been reassured. Moreover, her therapist would have known about her fears and positive expectations, and not alienated her, which the wrong interpretation he had offered had succeeded in doing.

The second example was a dream which the dreamer had had on a number of occasions for many years. The dreamer had recently completed her training as a psychiatric nurse. The dream is as follows:

The stalker

> There is an old castle with a central courtyard. I am three storeys high on an external stone landing that runs around the outside of the building. I am running away from a man who is chasing me. Part of the pathway ahead of me has collapsed. There are stones lying around. I am trying to make my way past the broken part of the landing by walking close to the building.

If we examine the dream from the point of view of an analogy or metaphor for the way she sees something happening in her life, then the dream obviously relates to a recurring anxiety that she has. The dreamer is under stress from two sources: her unknown pursuer and the collapse of the pathway ahead of her. The fact that this dream has repeated itself for a number of years indicates that either a particular situation keeps recurring or that the dreamer has a characteristic way of perceiving challenging situations.

In either case the dream gives a picture of how this dreamer sees herself reacting in certain situations which straightforward questioning would not reveal. The dream is not only an accurate metaphor of a given situation in the dreamer's life, it also presents the therapist with a powerful metaphor that can be used in the client's therapy, as will be demonstrated with the next dream.

The third dream is also a repetitive dream, one that used to be enjoyable for the dreamer, but had recently changed and taken an unpleasant turn. The dream is as follows:

The dream pony

I find the pony which I used to have when I was young and on which I won many riding events. I again mount the pony wondering if it has retained its racing ability. To my joy and surprise it has still got its ability.

The dreamer recalled having had this dream on a number of occasions at intervals of up to one year. Some months ago he had again dreamed about his pony, but the dream had changed:

The dying pony

I find my pony in a neighbour's field. The pony is dying. There is nothing I can do to save it. I feel a great sense of loss.

The dreamer, when a small boy, was given this pony by his father. It was by far the best of a series of ponies he had throughout his childhood. He was very successful in winning competitions with it and very much regretted when his father sold the pony because he had got too big for it.

From what the dreamer had said about the pony being associated with achievement and personal success it seemed likely that the first dream metaphorically reflected periods of his life when the dreamer had surprised himself by rising to some challenge.

Information was elicited from the dreamer that supported this explanation. He also said that he was undergoing changes in his career, and that he felt insecure since he was now only employed part-time and doubted that he would ever succeed in obtaining full-time employment in his new chosen career. The change in the dream can be clearly seen as a metaphorical representation of his introspected self-doubt. Again these dreams give a vivid picture of the dreamer's predicament that a word description on its own could not display. Furthermore, the powerful personal metaphor of the pony could be used in many ways to help the person find the personal resources needed to make the best of the possibilities within his present situation. It would be important to note in this case, for example, that the pony is not dead, and that, should the dreamer find the personal resources to rise to his present challenge, he might well find himself rediscovering his pony, healthy and strong, in a future dream.

We can see why it is important to be aware that dreams may, in the absence of accurate information, actually exacerbate a client's problems, either through the therapist's or the client's misinterpretation of the dream or because the dream images may themselves arouse anxiety in the client. Children may be afraid to sleep or, indeed, to be left on their own, because of a fear generated by a nightmare. The nightmare may have been prompted by the child's waking thoughts about a particular situation in his life which needs to be addressed. Equally, though, the nightmare may be a metaphorical translation of a traumatic episode seen on television. Whilst watching a traumatic incident on television the child may feel a degree of control. Perhaps he can choose to watch it or not, or he may have company with him while he is watching it. When it comes to our dreams, however, we have no such sense of control. We know that the nightmare comes when we are on our own, in the dark. Even more terrifying, it comes from within our own mind. Little wonder then that this invasion of their private psychic space can lead children to a fear of sleeping or a fear of dreaming the nightmare again.

A young man came to see me who had been attending psychoanalysts for a number of years for the treatment of a hand-washing compulsion and making no progress. He told me that one day, some years earlier, before his problems began, he had gone for a swim in the local swimming pool. In the water he found the floating dead body of a man. Following this incident he was haunted by two nightmares:

Horses' heads

It is dark. I am surrounded by the heads of horses. There is no escape. I feel terrified.

The hourglass

I am watching the sand falling in an hourglass. I can hear horses breathing all around me. I feel terrified.

Why should he be surrounded by horses' heads and why should this image terrify him? The experience of seeing the dead body in the swimming pool was obviously deeply disturbing for the boy. He would naturally have introspected about it. These emotionally arousing introspections would have given rise to traumatic dreams or nightmares about the incident. His first nightmare may well represent a fear of having those nightmares about the dead body. The horses' heads may actually stand for the nightmares themselves. The horse's head, or shall we say the mare's head, is an apt symbol for nightmare. The fact that he only sees the heads draws our attention to the fact that these mares are 'head-mares' rather than events in the real world. That he is surrounded by them shows that he sees no escape – every day is rounded by sleep in which the nightmares can return.

The second nightmare develops as a result of a further fear, that of dreaming about the horses' heads. The hourglass signals that time is passing. The hour of sleep and the nightmare is approaching. This is indicated by the sound of the horses' breathing. In other words the hour of sleep approaches and the nightmare can already be sensed breathing down his neck. This dream then can be seen to represent his wakening fear of sleep time approaching and the occurrence of the terrible nightmare of the 'horses' heads'.

It is immensely reassuring for a client to learn the logical basis for his nightmares and so it was with this young man. His hand-washing compulsion can also be seen to have arisen in reaction to the same traumatic event. The washing of his hands was the washing away of any contamination from the dead man.

Repetitive dreams

Repetitive dreams often produce anxiety. With the dream of the horses' heads we can see how, if the person reflects on the feared nightmare, and if those reflections arouse further fear, then the structure of the nightmare changes. In that example the nightmare clearly changed to a nightmare reflecting the fear of having a nightmare.

Many repetitive dreams, however, maintain their format no matter how many times they are dreamed. In these instances, we are seeing a recurrence of the same waking emotionally arousing introspections.

The following couple of examples are from my own childhood:

The Kidnap Nightmare

I am walking down a road in the village where I was born. I am about twelve years old. Suddenly a gypsy caravan appears and a gypsy leaps from the caravan and chases me. He catches me and takes me away with him. I am terrified.

The dream was inspired by an incident which occurred one day when I saw some gypsies passing our gate and I shouted 'gypsies' at them. One of the gypsies started to run towards me and I ran away terrified that he would catch me. The dream is an obvious replay of my introspected fear of being kidnapped. The location and appearance of the caravan and the gypsy were changed, as we would expect. In the dream, a gypsy actually takes me captive – a fear that frequently recurred whenever I saw gypsies following the name-calling incident. Hence the recurrence of the nightmare.

The money nightmare

Money, in the form of coins, is pouring from the sky. I am filling a bucket with money as fast as I can but the ground keeps cracking open beneath my feet and I have to keep jumping onto safer ground to avoid falling into the holes.

This nightmare is an accurate metaphorical representation of a childhood concern of mine. I was raised as a member of a large, strict, Catholic family in rural Ireland in the 1950s when money was scarce. I sometimes daydreamed and even prayed that I might come into a fortune. I would then feel guilty that this fantasy was incompatible with the religious beliefs I was being taught. I recall praying that I would discover the legendary 'pot of gold' at the end of the rainbow – the money from the sky. This immediately aroused guilt that such selfish prayers might cause me to be sent to hell, hence the cracks in the ground into which I was in danger of falling.

There are a number of ways to help a client resolve fear associated with anxiety dreams. The first thing is to look at the dream as a metaphor for how the client feels about some anxiety-provoking event in his life. Usually the dreams clients bring to therapy are recalled because of their dramatic and emotional intensity. Often the parallel between the dream and current events in their lives are quite obvious. In such instances, resolving the underlying issues will also, of course, remove the need for the anxiety dreams.

Sometimes working on the nightmare itself is advisable. Here again there are several avenues of approach. One is to have the client imagine replaying the dream on a screen while helping him stay calm and relaxed. The client may find this easier if he speeds the film up so that it appears to last only moments. This helps him dissociate from the imagery which reduces the feelings of anxiety. The client can also be asked to imagine stepping into the film after the incident is over and to imagine that everything goes backwards in time very quickly to before the frightening incident started. This process may need repeating several times and usually results in a dramatic reduction in fearful feelings.

Another approach is to have the client interact with the feared situation. The client can imagine, for example, bringing whatever resources he needs into the scene to enable him to handle the feared situation more effectively. This is particularly useful with children whose nightmares may have been inspired by some traumatic television viewing.

Dream paralysis

Because REM sleep is accompanied by a paralysis of anti-gravity muscles, if someone wakes up before coming out of REM sleep they may be badly frightened. This can lead to a fear of going to sleep. When the client understands that this is a naturally occurring paralysis that will spontaneously end within moments of waking up they may be greatly reassured.

Pre-cognitive and telepathic dreams

One of the questions I am frequently asked when I lecture on dreams is whether dreams can predict the future. The occurrence of pre-cognitive dreams is a controversial issue amongst sleep researchers. We can see how, if dreams are frequently based on our anticipations of the future expressed metaphorically, they might come to seem to be prophetic. For example, if we are afraid that our mother might die because she is old and fragile, she is likely to be replaced in our dream by someone who is also old and fragile whom we dream has died. Not surprisingly, on some occasions, such a dream may actually come true.

This dream clearly does not require a pre-cognitive explanation in the sense of the dreamer having access to paranormal information. However, there is a great deal of anecdotal evidence of people dreaming future events that do not concern them personally. Such accounts, although not scientific, can be impressive (Inglis 1987). Reports of psychic premonitions are not, of course, confined to dreams; they are also reported from waking states. There is no inherent reason why, if such phenomena exist, they should also not occur during dream sleep. One's reaction to this evidence is inevitably going to be decided in part by one's view of psychic phenomena in general. The only dream experience that I personally recall that may have some psychic connection is the following dream.

The coffin nightmare

I am visiting friends of mine in their home. The husband is at work. I am talking to his wife when the phone rings. Putting the phone down she informs me rather casually that she has just learned that her husband has died at work. His body would be arriving at the house shortly. Sure enough, moments later, her husband's body arrives in a van and is carried into the house in a cardboard coffin. I am horrified since it seems likely that the coffin may burst open at any moment.

The dream occurred following a meal with friends in a restaurant the previous evening. I had just finished teaching a seminar in England and we were having a relaxing conversation over dinner. One of my friends mentioned casually that a friend of his, who was also an acquaintance of mine, was dying. I was rather surprised at the casual way he mentioned this shocking news. The first part of the dream can be seen as a metaphorical acting out of that surprise. I was puzzled by the second part of the dream involving the cardboard coffin. Later, on returning to Ireland, I told my wife the dream. "That's rather odd," she said, "because that day I had been rather appalled to hear a news item on the radio about cardboard coffins." Was there, we both wondered, a telepathic element to my dream?

The book which did most to arouse public interest in the possibility of having dreams which foretold the future was J W Dunne's (1927) *An experiment with time*. Dunne kept a dream diary and noted many dreams which appeared to foretell future events. Perhaps the most curious aspect of Dunne's research was that the glimpses of the future which he appeared to see in his dreams for the most part were concerned with insignificant details. (In one dream, for example, he saw an umbrella, unsupported, standing upside down on its handle outside the Piccadilly Hotel. The next day he saw an old lady walking towards the Piccadilly hotel holding a similar umbrella upside down, pounding its handle on the pavement.) But Dunne recorded so many of these events that he felt that chance coincidence was an unlikely explanation.

One possible explanation for the insignificance of the details, I suggest, is this: because a waking concern has to find metaphorical clothing for the dream, some detail from the future, if available to the dreamer, might well be incorporated into the manifest structure of the dream if it can play a part in expressing the concern analogically.

A researcher who has taken an experimental scientific approach to psychic phenomena in dreams is Professor Montague Ullman (1974) the founder of the dream laboratory at the Maimonides Medical centre in New York. In a series of scientifically controlled experiments Ullman produced significant evidence that telepathy can take place in dreams. In a typical experiment a subject would concentrate on a randomly selected painting and to try to get another subject who was asleep in an adjoining room to dream about it. On some occasions the experiments succeeded and on some occasions failed. Over a series of fifteen trials the number of hits exceeded misses such that the odds of the results being due to chance were calculated at a thousand to one. Whilst most scientists are willing to concede the possibility of extrasensory perception, they feel that insufficient scientific evidence exists, as yet, to validate these phenomena.

If we were to entertain the possibility that such phenomena do occur, how could we go about explaining them? One possibility might be that the brain can communicate with reality beyond time and space, a form of subtle direct perception. In which case, indications of such possibilities may arise somehow in dream states. But that does not necessarily mean they have to be concerned with anything of significance in themselves. Such details from the future would simply be used by the brain to metaphorically represent a waking concern of the recent past.

On the face of it the following example, because of its unlikely nature, seems impossible to explain other than by pre-cognition. It was experienced by a friend of mine one cold winter in southern England.

The lizards

Our house was invaded by lizards. They seemed to be everywhere, wherever we looked, under chairs, under the sofa, behind cupboards. Some were alive but some were dead. It was very disturbing.

The dream was so vivid that my friend discussed it with his family and at work. He had seen lizards on holiday around the Mediterranean but never in England and experienced the dream as a very odd one indeed.

It was winter time and, one week later, his family awoke and found, to their amazement, the dream had come true. There were lizards and bits of lizards in the kitchen and several rooms. Some were moving slowly, some had tails missing, some were dead. They were all over the place and it took a while to find them all. The only explanation for it seemed to be that the family cats had found a nest of hibernating lizards and, throughout the night, had brought them into the house through the cat flap.

In this case the dreamer had been expecting a visit from people he held in low regard and whom he had even thought of as "a lower life form". Perhaps his brain, in search of a metaphor to express this troubling intro-spection, accessed this 'ready-made metaphor' from the future and used it in the dream. But this metaphorical explanation would need to be seen as applicable to a wide range of pre-cognitive dreams before we could confidently offer it as a general explanation of such phenomena.

If such psychic phenomena can reliably be shown to occur during dreaming how would they impact on my theory? We have seen how the PGO signals that are released prior to and during REM sleep are in fact orientation responses anticipating new stimuli and that, because information about what is happening in the environment is inhibited, the organism responds to these signals by releasing the patterns of arousal that have not yet taken place. If at some level there is paranormal information about the future available to the person, it might well be expected that this would be released in the context of the REM state since, as we have seen, this state is actively anticipating the arrival of new information.

Lucid dreams

Lucid dreaming is a subject on which we can be more definite. Throughout history there are reports of people who claimed to have been conscious of being in a dream. This phenomenon was studied in the laboratory by Stephen La Berge (1985). He got subjects to give a predetermined signal of when they were dreaming. The signal consisted of blinking their eyes during REM sleep, since other muscles are paralysed. Having a firm intention to become aware that one is dreaming prior to going to sleep can increase the chances of a lucid dream as can practising certain forms of self-suggestion over time. Even so, lucid dreaming is still a fairly volatile and rare phenomenon, even for those who have experienced it.

Hopes have not been realised for dream researchers wishing to make lucid dreaming more accessible, thus providing not only a means of creating exciting fantasies, but a potential means of, for example, deconditioning fears. Perhaps they are overlooking a means of achieving this outcome that's been around for centuries – hypnosis.

Hypnosis and dreams

Hypnosis may in fact be a direct route to accessing the dream state. The dream can be thought of as a 'reality simulator'. We have seen that, in the dream state, introspective thoughts are clothed in metaphorical sensory garb. We have also seen that the dream is a script inspired by a waking scenario that, in the REM state, is translated into a rich sensory scenario. This theory therefore allows us to separate the content of the dream from the state of mind in which a dream occurs. It may well be that the hypnotist's words are, in a sense, replacing the dream script and then turned into a sensory reality for the hypnotised subject. Anyone who has seen a stage hypnotist suggest to a hypnotised subject that a sweeping brush is a beautiful woman will have little doubt of the reality of the sensory impression thus created. This situation is almost identical to a waking thought being transformed into a sensory reality in the dream.

A hypnotised subject can be given a story and asked to dream a dream about it. The subject will report a metaphorical version of the story – just as occurs in dreams. Hypnotised subjects often show an uncanny knack of translating another person's dream back into its waking meaning. We would not expect the brain pattern of a hypnotised subject to be exactly the same as in the REM state since the state is not induced by the lower brain stem. Rapid eye movements similar to those that occur during REM sleep can sometimes, however, be observed in subjects whilst they are in a hypnotic state. Both states have similar EEG brain patterns.

The methods of accessing a hypnotic state can also parallel the way the REM state is triggered. The most common way to induce hypnosis is through a relaxation induction similar to how we access stage 1 sleep which is almost identical to the brain wave pattern in REM sleep. We saw that this was the state in which Kekule had his dream and in which Silberer did his research. The REM state is preceded by the firing of the orientation response, the PGO spikes in mammals. Shock or surprise, for example by suddenly jerking the subject's head down, is a standard stage hypnotist's method of inducing hypnosis. This method of course triggers the orientation response. A further method is to fixate the subject's attention, often on the hypnotist's voice or on an idea or a sequence of imagery. The key hypnotic skill is to limit the subject's attention to a specific train of stimuli. Here again we are paralleling what happens in the dream. In the dream the dreamer's attention is focused exclusively on the dream reality; no other point of view is perceived.

Trance logic

Trance logic has long been recognised as an important characteristic of the hypnotic state. It was defined by Weitzenhoffer (1989) "as an extreme tendency of subjects to rationalise any occurrence they experience, no matter how improbable or absurd it may be". He gives the example of a subject told to close the window in a room that is uncomfortably warm and who will do so with the explanation that the room is cold or draughty. Trance logic is regarded by some investigators to be one sure sign of the presence of hypnosis. Trance logic can also occur in dreams. I will give two examples. The first comes from one of my own dreams followed by a dream on a similar theme told to me by my brother.

The dead arose

I am talking to someone in a house when my sister walks in. I am surprised to see her since I know she is dead. The thought immediately occurs to me that this must be a dream. I reflect to myself, that, even if it is a dream, I can still enjoy the feeling that she is alive since the feeling of her presence is so real. My sister goes on to give an explanation of her miraculous return to life. She tells me that she was not really buried in the grave following her death, that it is hospital policy to hold on to dead bodies for further experimentation. It was, therefore, an empty coffin that was buried. When the hospital researchers were doing further tests on her dead body, she had started to breathe again. They had to keep these facts secret until now (some twelve months after her death) because they were waiting for her to regain strength. I accepted this explanation of her return to life as perfectly plausible.

The previous day, looking at a photograph of my dead sister, I thought I could sense her presence as though she were still alive. The dream can be seen as an acting out of my introspection from the previous day. My sister can appear as herself in the dream because her body was changed from a dead one to a live person. Her appearance in the dream triggers an awareness that I may be dreaming. Trance logic resolves the dilemma. My sister gives a preposterous explanation to account for her improbable return to life. Because of trance logic this explanation is fully accepted by me in the dream. I told this dream to my brother and he said that he had had a similar dream a couple of days earlier.

My brother's dream

My sister walks into the room. I am surprised to see her. I immediately think that I must be dreaming because my sister is dead. I then think to myself that it can't be a dream because I wouldn't question the reality of a dream reality. I therefore conclude that my sister is alive.

Here again we see the similarity between dream logic and trance logic. He says to himself that, because he is able to question the reality of the dream, it therefore is not a dream and he accepts the improbable reality of his dead sister being alive again.

One of the most remarked on facts about dreaming is that, despite spending about two hours a night doing it, we recall very few dreams and it is relatively unusual to do so unless we train ourselves to recall them (and even then most dreams are still forgotten). Some people are so good at forgetting their dreams that they even come to believe they don't dream at all. Most people, however, have experienced remembering one on waking only to forget it a few moments later. It seems that, once the dream work is done, we have no need to remember our dreams.

Forgetting, or amnesia, is also associated with hypnosis. Most good hypnotic subjects have the experience of coming out of a trance surprised to learn that more time has elapsed than they thought and recalling little of what actually happened in the trance. If, however, the person wakes up from the dream state gradually, paying attention to their introspective processes, they will be much more likely to recall a dream. Conversely, if they wake up suddenly, for example, by a door bell ringing, they are more likely to have amnesia for the dream. Similarly with hypnosis; any sudden switch of attention will facilitate the amnesia for what took place in the trance. But when the hypnotic subject has amnesia for what took place, any posthypnotic suggestions given in the trance will still be triggered when the appropriate environmental events are encountered. Likewise with the theory of the REM state I have described; the instinctive programming which takes place in the REM state will be activated in the appropriate environmental conditions.

So the bizarre nature of hypnotic phenomena can make sense when seen as accessing the potential of the REM state. Interestingly, the late Dr Milton Erickson recognised the occurrence of the common everyday trance which occurs about every ninety minutes. During this state, which lasts about twenty minutes, the brain switches from left brain information processing to predominantly right brain information processing. Erickson discovered that this was a good time to give his clients suggestions because their attention could be easily fixated in this state. This made them more suggestible because, in order to counteract a suggestion, it is necessary to form multiple viewpoints of the suggestion. Erickson also discovered that this light trance state could easily be deepened into a more profound hypnotic state with appropriate suggestions.

Dr Ernest Rossi linked this periodically occurring trance state to certain ultradian rhythms (Rossi, 1986) which involve a switch from left brain functioning to right brain functioning for a period of about twenty minutes every ninety to 120 minutes. Interestingly, dream sleep also follows this rhythm occurring approximately every ninety to 120 minutes during sleep.

Hypnosis is a powerful therapeutic tool which has yet to become part of mainstream therapy or medicine. There are hundreds of scientific papers that document the incredible medical results obtained using hypnosis. For example, a colleague of mine, Dr Jack Gibson, has performed over 4,000 operations with hypnosis as the only form of anaesthesia. Amongst its many medical uses hypnosis can reduce blood loss during operations, speed up recovery, accelerate skin healing after burning and even 'charm' away warts and verrucas.

Hypnosis used in psychotherapy has proved equally powerful. I have myself, whilst carrying out therapy demonstrations, frequently removed lifelong phobias from people in as little as thirty minutes using hypnosis.

There is good reason to believe that the basic therapeutic agent in many forms of therapy is the unrecognised induction of therapeutic trance states which may make use of traditional hypnotic mechanisms such as age regression, age progression, dissociation, positive hallucinations etc. This is as true of cognitive therapy as it is of more obviously hypnotic therapies such as 'Gestalt' which may involve hypnotic phenomena such as asking the client to imagine having an hallucinatory conversation with an absent person (Yapko, 1992).

Perhaps the main reason for the reluctance to recognise the importance of hypnosis is the absence of a scientific theory that explains it. I believe the analogical dream theory put forward in this book may point a way towards a solution to this problem. We know that about twenty per cent of the population can readily access a state of deep hypnosis, where suggested realities become as real as dream realities, and they may well be literally accessing the reality simulator that is the REM state. Therapeutic suggestions given in this state can have profound effects on the mind/body system. The rest of the population has the ability to access lighter states of hypnosis which certainly involve more right brain activity and which show a lesser involvement of the REM state such as may occur at sleep onset. It is to be hoped that the amazing and powerful therapeutic potential of hypnosis will become more widely used as we develop further our scientific understanding of this phenomenon.

There are, therefore, many therapeutic uses to which this new understanding of dreams can be put. These include the fact that, although a person is conscious of the contents of their introspections, they may not have the objectivity to distance themselves from them sufficiently to perceive their influence on how they experience their life. The dream, when perceived as a metaphor, may provide that sense of distance and *realness* that enables the dreamer to see their situation with a new objectivity. It can further provide the therapist with an insight into the dreamer's situation, which verbal language would find difficult to convey. It also gives an honest perception of how the dreamer really feels. It can provide a powerful metaphor which the therapist may choose to use in his therapeutic intervention by reframing the implications of the metaphor so that it has a positive outcome. It also provides a new understanding of how nightmares can contribute to clients' symptoms.

The sense of wonder and of unknown personal resources which can be evoked in a client by discovering that a part of them has the ability in dreams to create powerful metaphorical visions relating to their problems should also not be overlooked. The analogical dream theory also has the potential to provide a scientific understanding of the phenomenon of hypnosis which may help to accelerate its therapeutic acceptance and further development.

To understand the origin, meaning and function of dreams is to realise that most dreams may be routine productions, whose goal is usefully accomplished though not consciously recalled. This need not blind us to the potential insights that can be gained from those dreams whose metaphorical productions are of such great beauty, bizarreness or dramatic intensity that they are propelled across the threshold of sleep into waking consciousness. On most occasions the bath can be allowed to empty without a second glance, but on those occasions when someone pauses to look, it may be that the baby is still left inside it.

AFTERWORD

I HAVE PUT FORWARD in this book a theory of dreams and REM sleep which integrates the apparently diverse biological and psychological facts together with the genetic and phylogenetic data. It provides, I hope, a new insight into human thinking and the special function of analogical and metaphorical thought in human affairs.

Perhaps we can see more clearly now that the origin of dreams lies in those emotionally arousing expectations that remain unsatisfied at sleep onset and whose analogical expressions in dreams deactivates their pattern of arousal, leaving the brain better prepared to deal with tomorrow's emotionally arousing experiences.

It is interesting to reflect that the diversity and richness, the profundity and the beauty to which human dreaming has given expression has derived from a process which evolved in the first instance to programme instinctive behaviour.

In the final analysis, human dreaming can be seen as a mirror that reflects back, in analogical sensory form, the unmanifested hopes, fears and reflections that occupied the dreamer's introspective life while they were awake.

Joseph Griffin (1997)

CAN YOU HELP?

Since publication of the first edition of *The Origin of Dreams* people in clinical settings have begun to use this new understanding about brain function and why we dream. It is proving very helpful, particularly with people suffering from anxiety disorders, depression and trauma. Others have applied it to their own dreams and claim that it is giving them greater insight into what troubles or inspires them. The European therapy Studies Institute (ETSI) would like further examples of the way people are using this new understanding in therapy and their private lives and would be pleased to hear from readers of this book.

Please write to the author, Joe Griffin, about your experiences working with dreams, care of;

ETSI,
Church Farm,
Chalvington,
East Sussex
BN27 3TD.
United Kingdom

ABOUT THE AUTHOR

Joseph Griffin was born in Ireland. He studied for graduate and post graduate degrees in psychology at the University of London. As a research psychologist, he became intrigued by the question of how evolution has shaped the human mind. As a psychotherapist his main concern is with what constitutes effective psycho-therapy. Happily he was able to combine both these interests in this book which is based on more than twelve years of research into the origin of dreams.

In recent years he has become well known to many thousands of health professionals throughout the UK and Ireland for his well researched and groundbreaking seminars on the way ahead for effective treatment of mental disorders.

He currently lives in Ireland with his wife and two daughters.

REFERENCES

Aserinsky, E. & Kleitman, N. (1953) Regularly occurring periods of eye mobility and concomitant phenomena during sleep. Science, 118, 273-274.

Blakeslee, T.R. (1980) The Right Brain. Macmillan Education Ltd., London.

Bogen, J.E. (1969) The Other Side of the Brain, 11: An Appositional Mind. Bulletin of the Los Angeles Neurological Society 34, 135-162.

Bruner, J. (1986) Actual Minds, Possible Worlds. Harvard University Press, Cambridge, Massachusetts and London, England.

Cohen, II. & Dement, W. (1965) Sleep: Changes in threshold to electroconvulsive shock in rats after deprivation of 'paradoxical' phase. Science, 150, 1318.

Crick, F. & Mitchison, G. (1983) The Function of Dream Sleep. Nature, 304, 111-114.

De Becker, R. (1968) The understanding of dreams and their influence on the history of Man. Hawthorn.

Dement, W. & Kleitman, N. (1957) Cyclic Variations in E.E.G. during sleep and their relation to eye movements, body motility and dreaming. Electro-encephalography and Clinical Neurophysiology, 9, 673-690.

Dement, W. (1960) The effect of dream deprivation. Science, 131, 1705-1707.

Dement, W. (1968) The biological role of REM sleep. A. Kales Ed., Sleep: Physiology & Pathology. Lippincott, 1969, 245-265.

Dement, et al (1967) Studies on the effects of REM deprivation in humans and in animals. In S.S. Kety, E.V. Ewarts & H.L. Williams (Eds.), Sleep and Altered States of Consciousness, Proceedings of the Association for Research in nervous and Mental Disease, 45, 456-468.

Dement, W. (1972) Some must watch while some must sleep. Stanford Alumni, Stanford & W.H. Freeman, San Francisco.

Dewson, J., Dement, W., Wagener, T.& Nobel, K. (1967) REM sleep deprivation: a central-neural change during wakefulness. Science, 156, 403-406.

Dixon, N. (1981) Preconscious Processing. John Wiley & Sons, Chichester, New York, Brisbane & Toronto.

Dunne, J.W. (1927) An experiment with time. Faber & Faber, London, 1969

Ebbinghaus, H. (1885) Memory: A contribution to experimental psychology. (H.A. Roger & C.E. Bussenius trans). New York: Columbia University Press, 1913

Erickson, M.H. (1980) The Collected Papers of Milton H. Erickson on Hypnosis (four volumes). E. Rossi (Ed.) New York: Irvington.

Evans, C.R. & Newman, E.A. (1964) Dreaming an analogy from computers. New Scientist, 419, 577-579.

Evans, C. & Evans, P. (1983) Landscapes of the Night. London, Victor Gollancz Ltd.

Furr, R. (1993) A Device is Not a Paradigm. The Psychologist, 6, 261-262.

Ferguson, J. & Dement, W. (1968) Changes in the intensity of REM sleep with deprivation. Psychophysiology 4, 380.

Foulkes, D. (1962) Dream reports from different states of sleep. Journal of Abnormal Social Psychology, 65, 14-25.

Foulkes, D. (1985) Dreaming a Cognitive Psychological Analysis. Lawrence Erlbaum Associates, New Jersey, London.

Foulkes, D (1978) A Grammar of Dreams, New York, Basic Books.

French, T. (1954) The Integration of Behaviour, 11: The Integrative Process in Dreams. Chicago, University of Chicago Press.

French, T.M. & Fromm, E. (1964) Dream Interpretation. New York, Basic Books.

Freud, S. (1953) The Interpretation of Dreams. *In standard edition of the complete psychological works of Sigmund Freud, J. Strackey, (Ed.), London. Hogarth Press.*

Goodenough, D.R. et al (1965) *Dream reporting following abrupt and gradual awakenings from different types of sleep.* Journal Personality Social Psychology, 2, 170.

Griffin, J. (1993) *The Origin of Dreams: did Freud and Jung get it wrong?* The Therapist, Vol. 1, No. l, 18-22.

Griffin, J. (1993) *The Meaning of Dreams.* The Therapist, Vol. 1, No. 3., 33-38

Griffin, J. (1996) *Dreams, Creativity and Psychotherapy.* The Therapist, Vol. 3, No. 4, 8-14

Hall, C.S. (1953) *A cognitive theory of dreams.* Journal of General Psychology, 49, 277-282.

Hartmann, E. (1967) *The Biology of Dreaming. C.C. Thomas.*

Hobson, J.A., Goldfrank, F. & Snyder, F. (1965): *Respiration and mental activity in sleep.* Journal of Psychiatry Research, 3, 79.

Hobson, J.A., McCarley, R.W. (1977) *The Brain as a Dream-State Generator: an Activation-Synthesis Hypothesis of Dream Process.* American Journal of Psychiatry, 134, 1335-1368.

Hobson, J.A. (1988) *The Dreaming Brain. Basic Book, Inc., New York.*

Hobson, J.A. (1989) Sleep. *Scientific American Library, a division of HPHLP, New York.*

Hoppe, K.D. (1977) *Split Brains and Psychoanalysis.* The Psycho-Analytic Quarterly, 46, 220-224.

Horne, J. (1988) Why We Sleep: The Functions of Sleep in Humans and other Mammals. *Oxford University Press, Oxford, New York, Tokyo.*

Hudson, L. (1985) Night Life, The Interpretation of Dreams. *Weidenfield and Nicholson. London.*

Hunt, T.H. (1989) The Multiplicity of Dreams, Memory, Imagination and Consciousness, 28-30. *Yale University Press, New Haven and London.*

Inglis, B. (1987) The Power of Dreams. *Grafton Books, London.*

Jouvet, M. & Michel, F. (1959) *Correlations Electromyographiques du Sommeil Chez Le Chat Decortique et Mesencephalique,* Chronique Comptes Rendus de la Societe Biologie, 154, 422-425.

Jouvet, M. (1965) *Paradoxical sleep – a study of its nature and mechanisms.* Prog. Brain Research, 18, 20-57.

Jouvet, M. (1967) Mechanisms of the states of sleep; A neuro-pharmacological approach. *Presented at the 45th annual meeting of, and published by, the Association for Research in Nervous and Mental Disease. 45, 86-126. New York.*

Jouvet, M. (1977) *Neuropharmacology of the sleep waking cycle. In: S.D. Iversen, L.L. Inversen and S.H. Snyder (Eds.),* Handbook of Psychopharmacology, 8. 233-293. New York. Plenum.

Jouvet, M. (1978) *Does a genetic programming of the brain occur during paradoxical sleep? P.A. Buser & A. Rougel-Buser (Eds.)* Cerebral Correlates of Conscious Experience, Amsterdam, Elsevier.

Jung, C. (1964) Man and His Symbols. *Ed. C. Jung, Dell Publishing Co. Inc., New York, 42-44.*

Jung, C. (1965) Memories, Dreams, Reflections. *New York, Vintage, 158-159.*

Khaldûn, Ibn (1967) The Muqaddimah. *Translated from the Arabic by Franz Rosenthal and abridged and edited by N.J. Dawood. Routledge & Kagan Paul.*

Karasov, W.H. & Diamond, J. (1985) *Digestive adaptations for fuelling the cost of endothermy.* Science, 228, 202-204.

Koestler, A. (1964) The Act of Creation, *Hutchinson, London.*

Lorenz, K.L. (1966) On Aggression. *Methuen, London.*

Maclean, P.D. 1982) Primate Brain Evolution: Methods and Concepts. *(Eds.) E. Armstrong & D. Folk, Plenum Publishing Corporation, 309.*

Masson, J.M. (1984) Freud: The Assault on Truth. *Faber & Faber, London.*

Maury, A. (1853) *Nouvelle observations sur les analogies des phenomenes du reve et de l'alienation mentale*, Ann. Med-Psychol., 5, 404.

Morrison, A.R. (1983) *A Window on the Sleeping Brain*. Scientific American, 248, 86-94.

Morrison, A.R. & Reiner, P.B. (1985) *A Dissection of Paradoxical Sleep*. McGinty, D.J., Drucken, C., Morrison, A.R. & Parmeggiani, P. (Eds.), Brain Mechanisms of Sleep. *Raven Press, New York, 97-110.*

Mourizzi, G. (1963) Active processes in the brainstem during sleep. *Harvey lectures series 58, 233-297.*

Ornstein, R. (1986) The Psychology of Consciousness. *Penguin, London.*

Peretz, L. (1993) The Enchanted World of Sleep, *Yale University Press, New Haven & London.*

Piaget, J. (1971) Biology and Knowledge, *Edinburgh University Press.*

Pribram, K.H. (1971) Languages of the brain: experimental paradoxes and principles in neuropsychology. *Englewoods Cliffs, N.J. Prentice Hall*

Roffwarg, H.P., Muzio, J. & Dement, W. (1966) *The ontogenetic development of the human sleep-dream cycle.* Science, 152, 604-618.

Rosen, S. (1982) *My voice will go with you*, The Teaching Tales of Milton H. Erickson, M.D. W.W. Norton & Co., New York & London.

Rossi, E.L. (1996) The Psychobiology of Mind Body Healing, *W.W. Norton & Co. New York, London.*

Schur, M. (1966) Some Additional 'Day Residues' of the Specimen Dream of Psychoanalysis. Lowenstein, R.M., Newman, L.M., Schur, M. & Solnit A.J., (Eds.), Psychoanalysis: A General Psychology – Essays in Honour of Hartmann, H., New York, International Universities Press, 45-85.

Shah, I. (1964) The Sufis. *The Octagon Press, London.*

Shah, I. (1968) The Caravan of Dreams. *The Octagon Press, London.*

Silberer, H. (1909) Bericht Uber eine Methode, gewisse symboliche Halluzinations – Erscheinungen Hervozurufen and zu beobachten, *J.B. psychoanalyt. Psychopath. Forsch., 513.* (114, 176, 460-61, 499, 645-8).

Silberer, H. (1951) *Report on a method of eliciting and observing certain symbolic hallucination phenomena.* Organization and Pathology of Thought, *translation and commentary by Rapaport, D. Columbia University Press, New York, 195-233.*

Snyder, F. (1966) Toward an evolutionary theory of dreaming. American Journal of Psychiatry, 123, 121-142.

Spearman, C.E. (1927) The Abilities of Man, their Nature and Development. *MacMillian & Co. Ltd., London.*

Strumpell, L. (1877) Die Natur und Enotchung Der Trame. *Leipoig.*

Ullman, M. (1959) The adaptive significance of the dream. Journal of Nervous Mental Disorder, 129, 144-149.

Ullman, M. (1961) Dreaming, altered states of consciousness and the problem of vigilance. Journal of Nervous Mental Diseases, 133, 529-535.

Ullman, M. & Krippner, S. with Vaughan, A (1988) Dream Telepathy (2nd Ed). McFarland, Jefferson, NC.

Vgyotsky, L.S. (1934) Thought and Language. Izd. AKAD. Pedagog. *Also translation Kozulin, A. (1988) The M.I.T. Press, Cambridge, Massachusetts, London.*

Vogel, G.W. (1979) A Motivational Function of REM Sleep. In Drucher-Collins, R., Shkurovich, M. & Sterman, M.B. (Eds). The Function of Sleep. *Academic Press, New York. 233-250.*

Walker, S. (1983) Animal Thought. *Routledge & Kagan Paul, London, Boston.*

Wallace, G. (1926) The Art of Thought. *Cape, J., London.*

Watzlawick, P. (1978) The Language of Change. *Basic Books, Inc., New York.*

Weitzenhoffer, A.M. (1989) The Practise of Hypnotism, *John Wiley & Sons, New York, Chichester.*

Yapko, M.D. (1992) Hypnosis and the Treatment of Depressions, *Brunner/Mazdel, New York.*

INDEX